Hawaiian Fishermen

Hawaiian Fishermen

Edward W. Glazier

Case Studies in Cultural Anthropology: George Spindler,
Janice E. Stockard, Series Editor

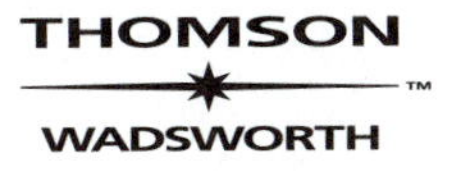

Australia • Brazil • Canada • Mexico • Singapore
Spain • United Kingdom • United States

Hawaiian Fishermen

Edward W. Glazier

Senior Acquisitions Editor: *Lin Marshall*
Assistant Editor: *Leata Holloway*
Editorial Assistant: *Danielle Yumol*
Technology Project Manager: *Dee Dee Zobian*
Marketing Manager: *Caroline Concilla*
Marketing Assistant: *Teresa Jessen*
Marketing Communications Manager: *Linda Yip*
Project Manager, Editorial Production: *Christine Sosa*
Creative Director: *Rob Hugel*
Executive Art Director: *Maria Epes*
Print Buyer: *Linda Hsu*
Permissions Editor: *Joohee Lee*
Production Service: *Sara Dovre Wudali, Buuji, Inc.*
Copy Editor: *Kristina Rose McComas*
Cover Designer: *Rob Hugel*
Cover Image: *Edward W. Glazier*
Cover Printer: *Courier Corporation/Stoughton*
Compositor: *Interactive Composition Corporation*
Printer: *Courier Corporation/Stoughton*

The logo for the Cultural Anthropology series is based on an ancient symbol representing the family: man, woman, and children.

All photos are reprinted with the permission of the author except where noted.

Cover Photo: native Hawaiian Fishermen and Surfers watch as a 196-pound ‘ahi is butchered for consumption by the ‘ohana (extended family) on Oahu, late 1990s.

Printed in the United States of America
1 2 3 4 5 6 7 10 09 08 07 06

Library of Congress Control Number: 2006921853

ISBN 0-495-00785-4

Thomson Higher Education
10 Davis Drive
Belmont, CA 94002-3098
USA

For my parents and theirs

Contents

Foreword

ABOUT THIS SERIES

The Case Studies in Cultural Anthropology Series was founded in 1960 under the joint editorship of George and Louise Spindler, both anthropologists at Stanford University. Since that time, more than 200 case studies have been published, and the series has enjoyed wide readership in college and university classrooms around the country and abroad. New case studies are published every year. With Louise Spindler's death in 1997, the series was left with one editor until Janice Stockard came on board in 2005. Janice is an accomplished author and brings powerful expertise in marriage, gender, family, and technology, as well as extensive editorial experience.

The case studies were initially conceived as descriptive studies of culture intended for classroom use. By design, they were accessible, short, and engaging. Their authors were anthropologists who had conducted extensive field research in diverse societies, experienced professionals who had "been there." The goal was to introduce students to cultural differences, as well as to demonstrate the commonalities of human lives everywhere. In the early years of the series, each case study focused on a relatively bounded community—a cultural group, tribe, area—that could be distinguished by its own customs, belief, and values.

Today the case studies reflect a world transformed by globalization and an anthropology committed to documenting the effects of the vast cultural flows of people, information, goods, and technology, now in motion the world over. In this twenty-first century, the greater pace and reach of globalization have created an infinite number of meeting points for people and cultures—and multiplied the sites and contexts for cultural change. In 1960 it was our task to present examples of the diversity characterizing the world's cultures; today it is our task to describe and analyze the impact of globalization on the diverse cultures of the world. To this end, we have recently published an anthology, *Globalization and Change in Fifteen Cultures: Born in One World, Living in Another* (2007), that focuses on the processes and impact of change on cultures represented in the Case Studies in Cultural Anthropology series.

In this series, we have set out to accomplish several objectives. One is to describe the distinctive features of the cultures of the world. Another is to analyze the sweeping changes underway, resulting from the processes of globalization, migration, urbanization, and modernization. Thus for anthropologists today, the task is both to document the cultural transformations and to decipher the ways in which the particular forms that change takes is influenced by the distinctive features of specific cultures. A no less daunting task is to understand the meaning of these changes for the people who live with them.

Globalization and cultural change in the twenty-first century present anthropologists with the challenge of studying (and writing about) extraordinarily complex processes. We invite you to experience this complexity in the current products of our series, as well as in the new anthology.

ABOUT THE AUTHOR

Edward Glazier grew up in the 1960s on the fall line just above the Delaware River, roughly 55 miles east of the Atlantic Ocean. This was close enough that he could detect a hint of the sea in the air during strong nor'easters but far enough that it kept him restless and eager for the drive to the beach in the back of his parents' station wagon. His Irish Catholic grade school and high school years were spent largely in anticipation of summers at the shoreline. So when it came time to choose a location for university studies, proximity to the ocean was a primary consideration. Edward found a stimulating intersection of sea and academics at the University of North Carolina at Wilmington, where he finished his B.A. in 1985 with a senior paper on dietary patterns among Algonquian tribes living along the North Carolina coast in the eleventh century. While pursuing his M.A. at East Carolina University later in the 1980s, he was invited to act as Field Director for Impact Assessment, Inc., an applied anthropology research firm then conducting a large study of the social and economic effects of the *Exxon Valdez* oil spill in Alaska. This ultimately became his thesis topic and led to employment with the firm at its home office in La Jolla, California. Ongoing interest in indigenous peoples and island societies led to additional graduate work at the University of Hawai'i at Manoa during the 1990s. Edward took a position as Sociocultural Specialist with the U.S. Department of the Interior, Minerals Management Service, in Alaska in 2000 but returned to Hawai'i to finish his doctoral work in 2002. Edward is now Research Director for the Pacific Islands Office of Impact Assessment, Inc., in Honolulu.

ABOUT THIS CASE STUDY

This case study is about fishermen who operate from small boats in the deep blue waters that surround the Hawaiian Islands. It is about Native Hawaiian and local fishermen for whom the sea is home, who persist in fishing despite the fact that it is at times not profitable and at times one runs at a loss. But as you will find in the reading, fishing has many rewards beyond the mere economic. In this day and age of megasupermarkets and online purchasing, it is refreshing to realize that real people still actually brave the elements to hunt, hook, and land our seafood. This book is about such persons and why they continue to fish in the challenging economic context of modern Hawai'i.

Edward Glazier has done a remarkably thorough ethnography, close to the fishermen and close to the sea. Sometimes this sea is calm as glass, sometimes rollicking and dangerous. But it is always there, a constant in the lives of the fishermen and on the horizons of all island residents. Some skippers with whom Edward worked have built their reputations as highly skilled and knowledgeable fishermen. They often take chances but not foolishly or capriciously. In Hawai'i, even among those captains whose trips reveal a recreational quality, there is much sincerity and focus. Invariably, the driving intent is to find and land big tuna, marlin, or mahimahi and to make it home safely—if only to market or consume the precious cargo!

When fish *are* found and landed, some part of the catch typically goes to the family larder or to share with others. But given the costs of boats, gear, fuel, and other expenses, every captain must fish with the market in mind. Some days, captain and crew may bring in hundreds of pounds and enjoy good prices at the marketplace. On those days, small-boat fishing is profitable. But, as is the way of fishing everywhere, many days are spent searching rather than catching, and profit is as elusive as the quarry.

So why fish? The answer is simple but serves to explain why many people around the world continue to work for themselves in challenging natural settings. That is, the activity, whether it is fishing, or hunting and gathering, or some form of craftsmanship or art, provides the opportunity not only to subsist but to do so freely and to form a meaningful identity, a meaningful life. Such activities and opportunities are best developed in a group setting in which the skills in question are mutually valued and arouse memories and understanding of a time gone by or of a time now passing rapidly.

Such is the case among fishermen in Hawai'i. The skills associated with fishing and plying the beautiful and dangerous waters of the Central Pacific are highly valued within the group and beyond. Those skills and underlying knowledge are hard won, and they hearken back to old ways of doing things. Significantly, they also tend to require attention to the sea-going challenges of the moment, rather than long-term economic vision in the modern world.

This study comes at a time of renewed national interest in the health of the world's oceans and its resources. Overfishing and use of certain fishing gear are often blamed for problems now apparent in certain fish stocks. But in the spirit of balanced thinking, fisheries managers and natural resource policy makers will do well to recognize that conservation and wise use of marine resources go hand in hand. For, as is made so clear in the details provided in this case study, fish and small-boat fishing have been and are critically important in the Hawaiian Islands. But we leave it to you, the reader, to discover what small-boat fishing in Hawai'i is; how it affects the lives of the participants, other island residents, and the marine environment itself; and how such understanding might influence the future of fishing in Hawai'i and maritime settings elsewhere in this rapidly changing world.

George Spindler and *Janice Stockard*
Series Editors

Preface

I ulu no ka lala i ke kumu

Passage of the National Environmental Policy Act (NEPA) in 1969 required that decision makers working in federal agencies address the human dimension—the effects people have on the environment and the way in which people are affected when some aspect of the environment is thereby altered. This was powerful precedent for a subsequent series of federal and state policies that recognized the place of human beings in the marine and terrestrial environment. Various agencies and programs have since developed to research and manage natural resources and their use by human beings.

Fisheries managers in Hawai'i and around the country and world are confronted with ever-increasing pressure on a finite base of resources in a complex sociopolitical environment. This has led to various strategies intended to conserve those resources while enabling fishing to continue in some regulated fashion. While it is critically important for the purposes of effective management to understand the dynamics of fish populations, ocean chemistry, and other physical aspects of marine fisheries, the most essential issues are human ones. The central issues are economic, social, and cultural. Without people fishing for a living, for fun, and for traditional purposes; and affecting the ocean and its resources in various ways, why and how would the biophysical sciences matter? Marine fisheries are best managed through consideration of the actions and needs of human beings.

But the human dimension is absolutely complex. People have to be seen as individuals who both create and respond to variable social conditions that in turn relate to the historical actions of others. Individuals also interact within and through many social groups, each of which may be seen in light of historical events and processes, and a contemporary context of globalizing political economies and rapidly advancing technology. Such are the intricacies confronting the social scientist, including the social scientist who studies people who catch, market, distribute, and consume seafood.

Aspects of fishing are similar everywhere, and persons familiar with the endeavor will undoubtedly perceive similarities between their own experiences and those described in this case study. But humans always act and interact in unique context, and the context of fishing in Hawai'i is one of unparalleled social, cultural, and genetic complexity. Yet the critical importance of fish and fishing in the Islands, and the likelihood that fisheries resource management will increasingly address and so call for deeper understanding of the human dimension mean the issues cannot be ignored. The following pages communicate a palapala hō'ike (report) on reconnaissance in this direction, focusing on the descendants of those who came to these Islands first and who continue to act in relation to centuries of history in Hawai'i. Descriptive attention is necessarily also given to the intricate society and cultural phenomena called *local* in Hawai'i.

It is my hope that other researchers might build on, improve, or at least consider aspects of this case study and these issues as they move toward a more comprehensive understanding of the complex human dimensions of marine fisheries in Hawai'i and elsewhere. There are lifetimes of work to be done in this regard.

The many fishermen and kupuna who granted access to their lives on and knowledge of the Pacific Ocean and its resources deserve the warmest mahalo nui loa, and this I humbly offer.

This work would not have been possible without the assistance, na'auao, and aloha of William Aila. He kanaka maika'i loa ia!

I am most honored to have had the opportunity to interact with George Spindler, Janice Stockard, and the editorial staff of Thomson Wadsworth in developing this case study.

Thanks also to Marc Miller of the University of Washington, Department of Marine Affairs and Shankar Aswani of the University of California at Santa Barbara, Department of Anthropology; both of whom were involved in the small-boat fishing studies funded by the Pelagic Fisheries Research Program at the University of Hawai'i at Manoa.

Mahalo too, to Craig Severance, University of Hawai'i at Hilo, Department of Anthropology, and Libby Stevens, both of whom provided invaluable insight and editorial assistance during the course of this project.

Finally, I also wish to express my gratitude to the following persons, each in some manner instrumental or influential in helping me live and work in Hawai'i, understand ocean culture, and/or complete the research described herein: Kiyoshi Ikeda, Luciano Minerbi, Herman Tuiolosega, John Petterson, Alani Apio, Samuel Pooley, Peter Manicas, Walter Ikehara, Lauren Morawski, Marcia Hamilton, Ulalia Woodside, John Sibert, Kitty Simonds, Michael Orbach, Donald Schug, Michael Hamnett, Judy Hamnett, William Puleloa, Reginald Kokubun, Athline Clark, Timothy O'Meara, Stewart Allen, Paul Dalzell, Cleveland Cowles, Herbert Barringer, Licia Dodie Lau, David Itano, Paul Bartram, Robert Humphries, Kimberly Lowe, David Hamm, Charles Langlas, Bud Greene, James Uchiyama, Georgia Niimoto, Raymond Firth, Paul Sensano, Vincent Shigekuni, Pouli Holookoaakala, Shanti Desai, Alex Almazan, Dorian Paskowitz, Skip Frye, Barry Kanaiaupuni, Tom Pohaku Stone, Michael Harbowy, Scott Strom, John Tucker, John Batson, Pembroke Nash, Joseph Grotolla, Phillip Jarrell, Steve Lane, Chris Tilghman, Will Allison, Phillip Thompson, Thomas Loftfield, R. Dale McCall, James Sabella, Jeffrey Johnson, Michael Weinstein, Laura Edles, Jonathan Wish Stevens, Edward Glazier, Sr., and Katherine M. Glazier.

Many persons assisted the development of this work, but any shortcomings or errors in description and analysis are solely my own.

A Brief Guide to Pronunciation

The reader is referred to authoritative sources for pronunciation of words in Hawaiian (e.g., Pukui and Elbert 1986). This brief guide is intended merely as a quick tutorial for the vernacular words and phrases presented in the following pages. Hawaiian vowels are as in English: a, e, i, o, and u. But they are pronounced as follows: "a" as the *ah* sound in papa; "e" as the *ay* sound in play; "i" as the *ee* sound in need; "o" as used in sole; "u" as the *oo* sound in moon. Diacritical marks are used to indicate stress on particular vowels and as glottal stops. The macron (called *kahakō* in Hawaiian) is used to stress and elongate any of the vowel sounds. For example, the ā sound in pāhoehoe (sheet lava) is stressed and lengthened, as in p*ahh*-ho-ay-ho-ay. The reverse apostrophe (called an *okina* in Hawaiian) is used as a glottal stop, as in the closed throat sound that should precede formation of the oft-used word ʻahi (pronounced *ah*-hee); or between sounds, as in Punaluʻu (pronounced poonahloo-oo). Certain vowel combinations (diphthongs) are also pronounced in a manner dissimilar to the way they are pronounced in English, with stress on the first vowel. For instance, the "ou" sound in Hawaiian is pronounced with stress on the "o," as in pouli (Hawaiian for eclipse, pronounced p*oh*-lee). Pronunciation of consonants is as in English, although the "w" is sometimes pronounced as an unstressed "v," as in Kahoʻolawe (one of the Main Hawaiian Islands, pronounced kah-ho-oh-lah-*v*ay).

With regard to pronunciation of pidgin in this context, again, the reader is directed to more authoritative sources. I offer a self-formulated guide to concepts, words, phrases, and accents encountered in the field.

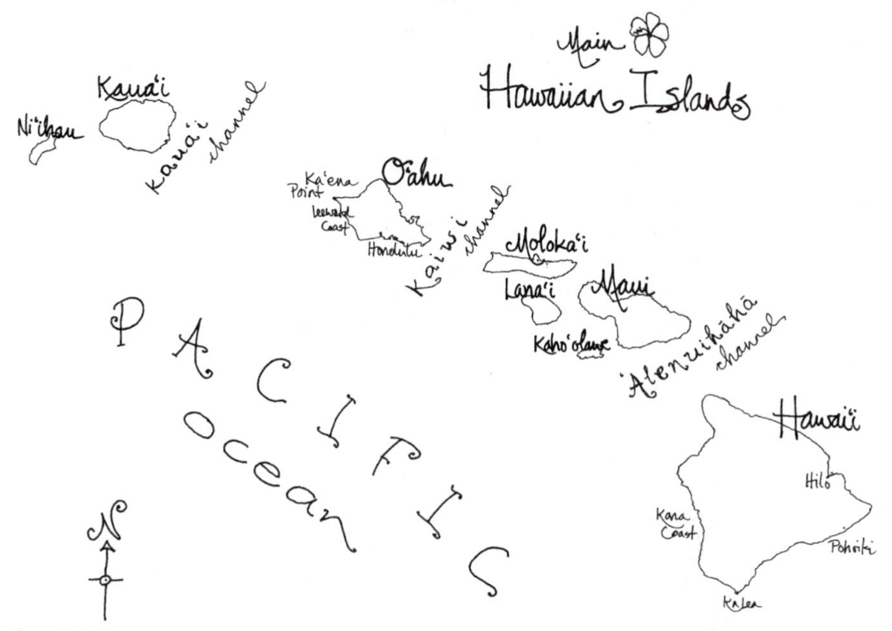

Source: "Art by Libby M. Stevens"

1/Introduction

According to oral traditions, Polynesians emerged from Kahiki, the land beyond the horizon. They are said to have arrived on the shores of Hawai'i in the far depths of time. Archaeological evidence indicates arrival by at least the fourth century A.D. Both linguistic and archaeological evidence indicate early colonists traveled to Hawai'i from the Marquesas Islands (Kirch 1985). In any case, intrepid Polynesian mariners reached Hawai'i following northbound oceangoing canoe voyages of well over 2,500 miles.

The navigational skills and feats of the Polynesians were like no other. Trusting their knowledge of the stars, currents, migrating birds, and the sea creatures that sustained them along the way, the voyagers reached Hawai'i at least four centuries before the Viking expansion into Britain and continental Europe. Their reasons for setting off into the unknown may always remain a mystery. But, one day, long into the voyage from Hiva Oa, the ancients finally discerned the rounded slopes of Mauna Loa and Mauna Kea, the largest mountains in the world measured from sea floor to summit. By easting the westbound North Equatorial current, travelers could eventually drift west to reach the lava-coated shores of Hawai'i. While the point of first landing is uncertain, it is quite possible the earliest mariners landed near what is now called Ka Lae (point or headland) in Ka'u District on the Big Island of Hawai'i, also known as Hawai'i Island.

Mauna Loa has coated the landscape of Ka Lae with its bubbling magma many times since the first colonists arrived in the region. Ka Lae itself is still a rugged and isolated area, little changed over the centuries. Modern-day residents live on a windy, lava-strewn landscape, punctuated with occasional patches of red clay, sparse ground cover, and stands of thorny koa haole and kiawe.

But the ocean at Ka Lae is as undeniably beautiful as the landscape is rugged, dropping as it does to purple-blue depths so close to shore that the open-ocean 'ahi (*Thunnus albacares* or Yellowfin tuna) can sometimes be caught with rod and reel from cliff side. Large holes were drilled into pōhaku (rocks) on the shoreline here centuries ago to serve as moorings for fishing canoes so people could drop their lines without drifting off in the strong currents. Modern shoreline fishermen[1] sometimes use kites or even inflated plastic bags to carry baited hooks into the deep waters that lay just beyond casting distance, not far from Kalalea heiau, a lava-rock fishing shrine situated above the deep waters southwest of Ka Lae.

The current that helped carry the early navigators to Hawai'i collides unceasingly at Ka Lae with waters moving southward under the force of dominant northeast trade winds. Groundswells are also part of the mix. These are typically northbound in summer, west and southbound in winter. During the winter months, massive swells, generated thousands of miles to the west and north of Hawai'i, march down along the Kona and Ka'u coasts, their long, textured walls sparkling in the strong, low latitude sun. Approaching shore, they rear up quickly from the depths to explode with great surging force, first above patches of offshore reef, then against the black pāhoehoe (sheet) lavas that fall off into the deep ocean all around western Ka'u District. The long voyage of wind-driven liquid energy ends with a roar and a hiss on the fine coral sands that fill the occasional coves and gaps along the rugged shoreline.

BEGINNINGS

My first visit to Ka Lae was during a particularly stormy period in the winter of 1997. The west-northwest swell was huge that day, and strong trade winds made for very choppy surface conditions. Sideways rain and sand pelted my back as I stood on the little beach facing southwest, toward distant Samoa. While peering through the rain and wind to observe the crashing surf, something on the chaotic southerly horizon caught my eye just briefly, then faded. Maybe it was the plume of a breaching gray whale, or merely a bit of foam lingering a moment before scudding across the surface. Although I stood safely back from the breakers, the 'ehu kai (sea spray) soaked my binoculars, face, and eyes; it was hard to be sure, but it seemed there was something there in the distance that didn't belong.

Then, again it appeared. I dried the binocular lenses, squatted down with steady elbows, and focused. The object appeared on the face of a large swell and again a few moments later. It appeared to be moving closer to shore as the minutes and sightings passed. It was hard to believe a boat could manage out there, but as time passed it became clear. A small craft would rise up on the heaving seas, then plummet into the trough, disappearing for a while from sight, then rising again, spray flying from its bow as it met the force of the swell!

It occurred to me that the little boat might be in trouble in these giant seas. My first thought was that the Coast Guard should be notified of a vessel in distress. But the nearest phone was way up the road, and it would take a cutter or chopper a long time to reach this lonely spot. I thought perhaps the captain had

[1]The terms *fishermen* and *fisherman* are used throughout this case study to refer to persons who fish in Hawai'i. While it is an empirical fact that small-vessel fishery in Hawai'i was historically, and continues to be, an enterprise in which males participate far more regularly than females, use of the terms is in no way suggestive that women were not or are not capable of the feats of males at sea. This usage is rather part of a personal decision to avoid use of the increasingly popular and politically correct androgynous term *fisher,* which I consider somewhat aesthetically displeasing and a less exacting descriptor for the Hawai'i case.

been pushed southward in the gale and was now trying to gain land while it was still within sight.

The craft slowly closed in on the shoreline. But there was no safe harbor here, and in fact the swells were exploding on a reef a quarter-mile from shore and reforming with plenty of leftover power to break again on the jagged rocks below. The small boat plodded onward nonetheless, ever closer to the zone of violent whitewater. Finally, the little vessel lifted high on the peak of an ominous grey-blue swell just seaward of the reef. I held my breath, so to speak, pending calamity. But at just that critical moment, the boat veered swiftly to starboard! Its port side was now exposed to shore just yards ahead of the white water, and for the first time the captain was visible, a dark-skinned man under the bright yellow of foul-weather gear. He appeared calm and in full control of the vessel, spinning the wheel casually from behind a windshield. There was no crash, no rending of vessel, and I suddenly felt foolish, realizing the purpose of the vessel and the skill of the captain. He was merely fishing, his troll lines now clearly visible as they teased the outer corner of the dangerous reef. Having passed the danger zone, the little craft continued for a bit on a rocking course parallel to shore, then turned seaward. Quartering the looming swells, the captain apparently began another circle along what I sheepishly decided must be a particularly productive fishing spot. Such was my first exposure to small-boat fishing and fishermen in Hawai'i!

In retrospect, the power of the ocean and gale was quite beyond anything I had previously witnessed in person, and misfortune was the only thing that made sense to me at the time. But research conducted since that day has made it abundantly clear that such skill and experience on the ocean are common among

Fishing heiau at Ka Lae, Hawai'i Island

small-boat fishermen in Hawai'i. Indeed, the vast Pacific surrounds every shoreline, and members of local society respect and reward those who learn its challenging ways.

A GLIMPSE OF LAULIMA

The gutsy captain of the small boat at Ka Lae had piqued my curiosity. In the spirit of the social scientist, I made some inquiries and learned he would arrive just east of the headland at little Kaulana Bay later in the morning. Entry into the harbor was skilled but uneventful, despite a maze of swirling currents and breaking surf on the west side of the channel. Once safely inside, two older men in baggy shorts, rubber slippers, and extra large T-shirts helped load the boat on its trailer. They had a dented old Ford F-150, ready and waiting. I started to approach the captain with a question about his trip, but he looked less than eager to talk and I thought better of it. Once the truck-to-trailer hook-up was completed, the captain moved a cooler from the boat onto the bed of the pick-up and drove off, with trailer chains and boat rattling up the bumpy road.

I ended up talking briefly with his helpers. Though not very talkative, the men revealed that Kaleo (pseudonym) had been fishing for two days and nights, and this was the third morning of his trip—furthering my amazement of his skills. One of the assistants called himself "da hah-bah-mast-ah," in the linguistically rich, intelligent, and ever-evolving local patois once known as Hawaiian Creole English, now "pidgin," or "local kine." He told me that he voluntarily helped local fishermen get in through the channel and up the ramp, and used a citizen's band radio to keep track of them while at sea. I'd previously met another elderly man who assisted fishermen in the same manner at a boat ramp up the coast. So, as it turned out, Kaleo's activities offshore were communicated to the harbor master throughout much of his trip. Should something have gone wrong, the situation would have been known and help quickly dispatched. In reality, Kaleo was not fishing alone but as part of a network of persons cooperating toward safety and success. This might be called laulima, or "many hands," in Hawaiian. I would learn much about this concept and process of kōkua (cooperation) over the subsequent months and years.

During the late 1980s, a proposal to improve the little harbor at Kaulana was ultimately rejected by a slim but vocal majority of residents. The proponents, some of whom lived in mauka (upland) portions of Ka'u District, felt convenience and safety of access could be improved, with heightened opportunities for commercial fishing. Other residents, many of whom lived closer to the ocean, felt that an improved facility could bring unwanted change, that it would alter the preferred "laid-back" local lifestyle and associated fishing activities.

Regardless of the rationale for resisting harbor improvements, the outcome of the referendum effectively helped to preserve the lifestyle of Ka Lae residents, which to this day is one with deep historic precedent—a small population of primarily Native Hawaiians living in geographic isolation, under conditions that call for relative self-sufficiency. This is similar to the lifestyle of many Native Hawaiians and other local residents of the larger Ka'u District as well, which itself is relatively isolated from many of the amenities and services many

Americans take for granted. But Ka Lae residents with whom I spoke claim to enjoy the rugged landscape, each other, and the simple way of life they believe is an extension of the way Hawaiians lived here in centuries past: fishing, gathering food from the ocean and shoreline, keeping livestock, and maintaining gardens. Like their kupuna (revered elders or forebears), people have adapted to the challenges, and many want to keep life as it is.

But there are problems here. There are serious implications associated with practicing this way of life in Hawai'i. There are pressures to change and a variety of factors that ultimately and insidiously catch up to further challenge those who resist changing. Some factors are obvious to the residents; others are not. These issues are central to this case study and to anthropological theory of social change, and I return to them repeatedly in subsequent chapters.

A CHANCE TO DO SOME FISHERIES RESEARCH IN HAWAI'I

Some months after that winter visit to Ka Lae, I was asked to work on a study that would examine and report on social and economic aspects of the small-boat fishing fleet in Hawai'i. The project was funded by the Joint Institute for Marine and Atmospheric Research, Pacific Pelagic Fisheries Research Program at the University of Hawai'i at Manoa (UH), as part of an ongoing effort to better manage fisheries resources in Hawai'i and elsewhere in the Pacific.[2] I was enthused to take part as I had done similar work elsewhere in the country in keeping with interests in maritime social science and a lifelong passion for the ocean and seagoing craft. Ocean experiences color the fringe of my memory, and just being in Hawai'i was fulfillment of a dream that started early in the 1970s while a novice surfer on the East Coast. Although a newcomer to the Islands in the 1990s, I had long been fascinated with Hawaiian surfing, Hawaiians, and the ocean in Hawai'i, and had listened to the tales of many friends who had managed to make the trip across the Pacific. Exposure to small-boat fishing at Ka Lae and the beauty of the ocean there and elsewhere in the Islands only furthered my enthusiasm for finding project work associated with my interests. The small-boat fishing study was an ideal opportunity.

STUDY RATIONALE

One objective of the project was to better understand in the Hawai'i context the typology that fisheries managers around the country typically use to conceptualize groups of fishery participants for purposes of research and regulation. Resource managers and policy makers working in state and federal fisheries

[2]The principal marine fisheries management entities in Hawai'i are the State Division of Aquatic Resources and, at the federal level, the Western Pacific Regional Fisheries Management Council (WPRFMC) and the National Marine Fisheries Service (NMFS). NMFS has a regulatory enforcement staff, assisted in some instances by the U.S. Coast Guard. The State's Division of Conservation and Resource Enforcement (DOCARE) handles regulatory enforcement in state jurisdiction waters. State jurisdiction waters extend from the shoreline to 3 miles offshore, while federal waters extend from 3 to 200 miles offshore.

agencies in the United States tend to characterize fishermen as either commercial (and part-time commercial), recreational, or subsistence/consumptive-oriented, with the subsistence classification thus far somewhat specific to Alaska or Native American groups in the Pacific Northwest. As relatively little had been written about small-boat fishermen in Hawai'i, or the nature of local fishing operations vis-à-vis these categories, I set out with two other social scientists to study local small-boat operations in this regard. As my associates moved on to other projects, I became long-term analyst and author of the final technical report for the study. That report has proven useful for characterizing the fishery, but it was quite lengthy and broad ranging, and needed an integrating principle to render it useful for a wider audience.

As discussed further along in this chapter, I ultimately chose to revise the description with a directed analytical focus on the history and current workings of small-boat fishing in Hawai'i, and the processes through which Native Hawaiians and other local residents have and continue to experience social change within and through this endeavor. While the participants themselves obviously are the real authorities on such issues, it was and is my hope that this case study will shed some light on the issues and the challenges they have encountered and continue to encounter in this new century.

RESEARCH METHODS, CHALLENGES, AND SOLUTIONS

It was decided early in the small-boat project that a standardized survey with fishermen on O'ahu and Hawai'i Island would be useful for documenting various aspects of fishing across a wide range of participants. Plenty of information about the small-boat fleet was compiled through that method, but there remained a significant gap in direct understanding about the social and cultural subtleties of small-boat fishing operations as enacted in the Islands. The situation called for direct participation in and systematic observation of those operations.

Getting on board fishing vessels in Hawai'i proved to be a challenge. Stories about malihini ("fresh off da plane") haole (foreigner or Caucasian) surfers getting punched out on O'ahu and Kaua'i in the '70s led to some initial anxiety on my part. But generally speaking, the fishermen were friendly and helpful once I got past the phase of mutual uncertainty that always confronts the social scientist working in a new setting. As discussed elsewhere in this case study, there *is* lingering mistrust on the part of many Native Hawaiians and locals about haoles, and a complex set of cultural and interethnic issues makes for an interesting and challenging research setting. But the main challenges to this part of the research were more universal in nature. That is, many fishermen just are not keen on someone they don't know tagging along, observing them all day. There are also concerns about how a stranger might behave at sea, because once past the harbor entrance, there is no turning back. It took persistence and sensitivity to make things work—for one haole boy to get on board with trusting local captains and crew.

I did succeed on my own in a few cases. But the assistance of intermediaries who understood and appreciated the research mission was essential in breaking the ice with some of the captains. Of course, this required hanging around long

Students listen and the author takes notes as the kupuna speak of days long past

enough to get to know the intermediaries too. Although I was originally unconcerned about focusing the research in any one harbor, and in fact sought to understand variation in fishing-specific activity between harbors, the process of getting to know informants and intermediaries well enough to trust me at sea ultimately led to focused and sustained effort in a single popular harbor on O'ahu. I also continued periodic work in communities along the Kona Coast of the Big Island, and occasional work on Moloka'i, Maui, and Kaua'i.

Over the course of a year or so, I really did gain acceptance at the harbor on O'ahu, to the point that I was unable to go on all the fishing trips I was invited to take! In some instances, this led to loss of respect for me and my job. But the demands of working full-time at this ethnographic enterprise and in a related research position left me no choice but to turn some people down. Some respect was regained when I became secretary of a local boat-fishing club, and this turned out to be an excellent way to better understand the lives of the fishermen and their families in a natural way and setting.

Of note, I did encounter some dangers during the course of the study. Although my primary informants were not involved with drugs, I was aware of the use of crystal methamphetamine (also known as ice or *battu*) at various places and times throughout my travels in the Islands. I steered clear of such situations as they were obvious—during use most users reveal a bloodshot stare and lolo (crazy) countenance. An underground economy is associated with "ice" and other illicit drugs in Hawai'i. The phenomenon is by no means specific to any given group, but rather, as is the case most anywhere now, there are places and situations in which awareness is warranted. My most trying field experience during this study was actually a side effect of "ice" abuse, and a case in which

I let my guard down, as related in the following summary field notes from research on Moloka'i in 1999:

> The kupuna I sought to interview was not at his residence, and so my friend and I decided to take a walk around the valley to gain a better sense of life in this remote area. A young local man sitting on the beach asked if he could catch a ride into town later on. He was still there waiting on our return. As he was friendly and unassuming, I gave him a lift. Our discussion was rich, as he was well-connected and knew much about fishing on the island. The road narrowed as it wound up a small pu'u (hill), forcing me to slow significantly. At that moment, a group of local men wielding automatic weapons jumped out in front of the car and forced me to stop! One approached my window and held a 9 mm handgun to my temple. He demanded, with much profanity, that we get out of the vehicle and lay face-down on the pavement. As there were no options, we did so, and for some time. At one point, I attempted to adjust my sunglasses, as they were grinding into the road. But I was warned that my next movement would be the last. Desperate, I glanced over at the hitchhiker and my friend to see how they were faring. Two of the men held the hitchhiker upright while a third secured his wrists with a sliding plastic cuff. I suddenly realized the assailants were actually undercover police officers. Upon questioning, the hitchhiker indicated that I had unwittingly assisted him and that I was not complicit in his own crimes. As I stood and brushed off my shirt, one of the officers offered an apology and explained that the young man was a fugitive ice dealer who had committed an act of arson on the other side of the island the previous day. Lesson learned.

A CHALLENGING TYPOLOGY

During early interactions with the fishermen at sea and around the harbors, it quickly became apparent that something was not quite right, especially in the Hawai'i context, with trying to classify fishermen as distinctly one type or another. I would go on a "commercial" trip, for instance, and it would turn out to become something else, or a combination of things. I met a few hard-core commercial captains, but these were the exception. This is described later. I have to say that I knew classification was a tricky issue through work in other areas of the country and through my own direct experience with fishing back in the mid-1980s. Back then, I sometimes assisted my late best friend with his "commercial" troll and gill-net operation in the waters off southeast North Carolina. There were lots of times we, or he, just kind of cruised, or went oystering, or did other kinds of fishing with the boat and gear, skipping the commercial sale part, as when prices were down or fishing was just so-so. There were times we fished just to get some dinner, and there were times when we didn't fish at all and the boat sat in the yard while construction work paid the bills. This flexible and less-than-hard-core fishing lifestyle is common among small-boat fishermen everywhere.

But the operational flexibility of captains and crew is especially clear in Hawai'i, and the unique local social context both enables and complements it. Generally speaking, many small-boat fishermen in Hawai'i continually move in and out of commercial fishing—even on a trip-by-trip basis. Some people definitely do stick with a solely commercial angle on a regular basis, but because all fishermen—on O‘ahu, at least—have the option of easily selling their catch at the fish auction in Honolulu, lots of factors enter into the overall disposition of the trip. If the catch is good and the price is right, selling some or almost all of it is typical. If the catch is just okay, more of it might be consumed and/or shared with others. Some people rarely sell and are sometimes termed recreational anglers. But with some sensitive questioning, these individuals often reveal an emphasis on a combination of fishing for recreation, and for eating and sharing. While observation makes clear that recreation runs through all types of fishing in Hawai‘i, and always has, fishing *just* for fun (as evinced, for example, in catch-and-release style of fishing) is a relative rarity here, at least among true locals. It is also clear that many of those who start out not selling their catch ultimately find themselves selling at least part of the take to pay for operating expenses. I assert, too, that fishing to eat runs through each of the accepted types. Virtually all locals consume or share at least some portion. In any case, any given local fisherman in Hawai‘i quite often may be classified under any one of the popularly used types. Even when people call themselves commercial fishermen, a little observation can prove otherwise.

I keep thinking of old Butch. He's the perfect example of a local guy who is all about fishing but who tends to defy easy characterization. He kept telling me he was a commercial fisherman, but I watched him do everything except sell fish over a period of many months. When he returned to selling with vigor later on, he would also share some of his catch. This is a single case but characteristic of many, and is perhaps the most valid illustration of the predominant opportunistic tendency in the Hawai‘i setting.

Fishermen in Hawai‘i tend to be opportunistic in other ways as well. This study is focused on small-boat troll fishing, but other traditional and novel boat fishing methods are also used. In reality, however, shoreline fishing and gathering are the most common ways in which residents harvest or attempt to harvest marine resources in the Hawaiian Islands. Indeed, thousands of enthusiasts on each of the main islands commonly participate in shoreline fishing activities, such as "whipping," "slide-baiting," "spearing," "poking," "throw net," and other methods of occasionally productive shoreline or nearshore fishing and gathering activities. Many boat fishermen also engage in these methods at times, most of which involve relatively little investment or operating costs.

Portraying the flexible and opportunistic nature of small-boat fishery participants in Hawai‘i leads to a basic dilemma. That is, the empirical situation tends to challenge one of the useful principles of social science—classification—and this was needed to help make sense of the mass of information about fishing and fishermen collected during the course of the small-boat project.

How to proceed? It occurred to me over the following months, and my perspectives have solidified over time, that for certain analytical purposes it might just be too difficult to confidently characterize many of the fishermen as distinctly one type or another, and that it was also probably better to look in a more flexible way at the fishing trips they took. I do not mean to suggest that categorizing cannot be done or has not been analytically useful in this setting. It can and has been useful to aggregate fishery participants in a standardized way and to analyze variation in their operations and behaviors—statistically, for instance.

Rather, my intent here is to more thoroughly understand and analyze the opportunistic and reactively flexible tendencies manifest in individual participants and operations.

I finally arrived at the idea that it would be better for my purposes to make the kind of fishing, rather than the kind of fisherman, the primary subject of classification and description. This would allow for valid description of the action in question and the way people tend to engage in it in a given time and place. Based on that description, I could then confidently explain the ultimate social consequences of fishing as it is commonly and variably undertaken in Hawai'i.

SMALL-BOAT QUESTIONS FOR DESCRIPTION, BIG SOCIAL ISSUES FOR EXPLANATION

My experiences at Ka Lae led to lots of basic questions about fishing in Hawai'i. Who were these guys who had so much "guts," who worked closely together to make it all happen safely, and who seemed to appreciate an ocean lifestyle so dearly? What kind of gear were they using? Where did they fish, and how, when, and why? What happened to the catch after the trips? What was the history of the fleet? Did fishing work differently in other parts of the Islands? How many people were involved? Were there conflicts between the various fleets? I feel fortunate to have had the opportunity to attempt to answer these and many other questions about this important aspect of life in Hawai'i.

Given the places I had been, the people I'd worked with, and my own experience and interests, there wasn't much question about how to organize and frame the descriptive results of the study. First, these would have to clearly relate the importance people attach to fishing and fish in this island setting, as this was the overarching finding of the work. If it was to be useful, the final analysis would also need to elucidate some of the ways in which marine resources are pursued and used in Hawai'i, and so improve the potential for effective resource management strategies in the region. Conversely, it would have to indicate the potential effects of those management strategies on people who pursue and use the resources on a regular basis. In these regards, the work would ideally contribute in some manner to fishery management plans and regulatory assessments required under NEPA and the Magnuson-Stevens Fishery Management and Conservation Act (Public Law 94-265). Finally, the analysis would need to address the implications of the fishing lifestyle for its participants. In this case, academic incentives and personal interests in indigenous peoples and social change led me to focus on the nature and implications of the fishing way of life for Native Hawaiians.

Hawai'i, like Alaska, provides an ideal setting for exploring ideas about social change and adaptation among members of indigenous society. Despite obvious dissimilarities in climate, there are notable parallels in lifestyles between Native Hawaiians and Alaska Natives[3] living in coastal regions of that

[3] I bring Alaska Natives into the discussion in part because I have had the opportunity in recent years to work with and recognize some of the issues encountered by various Native groups in that region.

state. Both groups have undergone terrific changes since Cook arrived on the respective shorelines. Today, many in both groups struggle with the result of that post-contact history and a modern ideology that remains partially focused on fishing and associated subsistence practices despite the modern demands of the predominant capitalist system. Indeed, the recent history of many Native groups in the United States reveals a continuing struggle in which the individual can be conflicted between an interest in traditional life ways and modern pressures to perform and compete in a capitalist economy. Historic events and processes and challenging contemporary conditions[4] further a situation in which Native peoples tend to find themselves at risk in an economic system that demands long-term attention to making and investing money, and the more the better.

I argue that this issue should not be taken lightly in that it may well relate to various social problems being experienced by indigenous persons across the United States. Native Hawaiians continue to experience disproportionately high rates of various social problems (e.g., Office of Hawaiian Affairs, Native Hawaiian Data Book 2002),[5] the male suicide rate among Alaska Natives is four times higher than that of the rest of the nation, and life on many Native American reservations is difficult at best (Goodluck and Willeto 2001).

That indigenous people continue to experience various social problems at a greater rate than other populations in the United States suggests that some macrosocial phenomena are operating wherein some groups benefit and others do not. One school of thinking holds that we have to understand the effects and consequences of historical processes and what it is about the way people interact in contemporary local sociocultural settings that leaves them with benefits or problems vis-à-vis the predominant capitalist system (Giddens 1984). This perspective may be particularly useful in this case in that Native Hawaiians (and other indigenous people in the United States) have undergone radical change in terms of land tenure, population structure, culture, and other critical factors, and they continue to be influenced by the effects of that history while adhering to various traditional life ways in a modern economic context.

The topical focus of this case study is most appropriate for examining these important issues. Fishing is an activity with extensive historical context for Native Hawaiians. It takes time and resources to accomplish; many people are involved; and as the analytical portions of this case study indicate, it can lead to a range of consequences for the participants.

While this case study maintains a focus on fishing among Native Hawaiians, it must be kept in mind that contemporary small-boat fishing in the Islands is not unique to that group. The indigenous people of Hawai‘i now live in island settings with many thousands of others, some percentage of whom fish from small vessels. These populations include local kama‘āina (island-born or long-term residents) of various ethnic ancestries, and malahini haoles (newly arrived

[4] Native Hawaiians are additionally challenged in that they have not yet benefited from tribal or nation status as recognized of Alaska Natives and Native American groups on the Continent.

[5] Year 2000 census figures indicate various challenges specific to my primary study areas, which are primarily Native Hawaiian. For instance, in the more urbanized study community, over 17 percent of families report conditions below the poverty level. The nationwide figure is 9.2 percent.

foreigners), also of various backgrounds. As of the year 2000, the State of Hawai'i was home to some 1.2 million persons; over 876,000 of those residents lived on O'ahu. As an indication of the massive changes that have occurred over the last century, only 154,000 persons lived in the Hawaiian Islands at the time of the 1900 census.

The history of the emergence of local society in Hawai'i over the last 100 years is one of great cultural and genetic interaction and resulting complexity. The plantation-era history of Native Hawaiians and immigrant groups is very much intertwined, with implications for the whole of local society in contemporary Hawai'i. Today (per the 2000 census that uses the term *race* to describe ancestral background), some 9 percent of persons reporting one race reported Native Hawaiian or other Pacific Island background. Some 42 percent reported a single Asian background, 24 percent reported being Caucasian, and 2 percent reported being African American. But significantly, over 21 percent of Hawai'i residents reported two or more ancestral backgrounds (the national average is about 2.4 percent), and nearly 7 percent reported three or more ancestral backgrounds.

Select aspects of sociodemographic and cultural amalgams are described in this case study, but the ultimate intent is to maintain an analytical focus on Native Hawaiian fishermen and the nature of living and fishing in a place where that heritage means something special. As members of the group with the longest tenure in Hawai'i, Native Hawaiians and part-Native Hawaiians are often ascribed unique status within local society. Locals are keen on knowing each other's background(s), and a claim to Native Hawaiian ancestry can be a

Prayer bundle near Kaena Point, O'ahu, 1999

Peddling fish at roadside, O'ahu

powerful statement about one's heritage and identity. At the same time, indigenous Hawaiians and other Pacific Islanders deal with a set of issues and factors that are unique within the larger society. As the following chapters illustrate in the context of fishing, for Native Hawaiians these relate to a tragic recent history on this 'āina (land) and a unique tendency to act with regard to culturally significant elements of that past and a deeper history.

2/Small-Boat Fishing in Hawai‘i

The Hawaiian Islands are the result of seismic and volcanic activity first occurring some 25 million years ago. By about 5 to 10 million years ago, an undersea mountain range nearly 2,000 miles long had been formed, the higher elevations of which now comprise the 6,450 square miles of shoals, reefs, and 132 islands of the Hawaiian Archipelago. Over the course of geologic time and through various evolutionary and biogeographic processes, a rich variety of plant, bird, and marine species had become endemic to Hawai‘i (Hawai‘i nei).

The islands of Ni‘ihau, Kaua‘i, O‘ahu, Moloka‘i, Maui, Lāna‘i, Kaho‘olawe, and Hawai‘i account for 99 percent of the archipelago's total land area. The islands and associated offshore zones contain complex land and marine ecosystems, including hundreds of species of interrelated algae, sponges, corals, segmented worms, mollusks, nudibranchs, crustaceans, bryozoans, echinoderms, tunicates, sharks, fish, rays, eels, reptiles, and mammals. There are, however, far fewer fish species in Hawai‘i than in tropical island locations further west and south in the Pacific. Islands in the Philippines, for instance, are home to more than 2,000 shore and reef fish species. Around 1,000 such species are endemic to the Marshall Islands. The isolation of Hawai‘i, along with its subtropical location, cooler water, and less sunlight, help to explain why only 450 nearshore and reef fish species reside here (Fielding and Robinson 1987).

The existing species do exhibit an array of color and activity. The coral reef is home to the major families of butterfly fish, surgeonfish (tangs), wrasses, damsels, blennies, gobies, scorpion fish, squirrelfish, triggerfish, parrot fish (uhu) and cardinal fish. Moving offshore past the fringe reef and volcanic outflows, the cerulean blues of the shallows become the indigo of great depths. All of the islands have their stretches of shallows and abrupt drop-offs, but deep water is closer to land in some places than others. On Hawai‘i Island, the 1,000 fathom curve is often within sight of land, while in certain places on O‘ahu, fringe reefs or stands of coral may extend miles out to sea, as is the case at Kaneohe Bay.

Underwater topographic features are of great importance to fishermen in the Islands, who often develop detailed knowledge of bottom conditions and the behavior of fish that congregate there or migrate in the upper levels of the water column. For instance, the mounded reef or underwater volcanic flow depositions called ko'a are known to attract pelagic and various inshore marine fishes and have been of interest to fishermen for centuries. The term *pelagic* refers to species inhabiting the upper layers of the open sea. In Hawai'i, the pelagic species of particular interest to the fleets include the various a'u (marlin) species, 'ahi (tuna) species, mahimahi (dolphinfish), and ono (wahoo). Areas of steep underwater contours and temperature changes are also targeted by fishermen, as fish wait in the depths to feed on bait moving from the shallows or on plankton-feeding creatures drifting in cold, upwelling currents. Of course, more transient features such as dead whales, ghost nets, and drifting logs also attract feeding baitfish and migrating pelagic species. Logs were and are of particular importance to fishing operations in Hawai'i, and knowledge of drifting materials is quite valuable and communicated across certain networks of fishermen, or just as often held close to the vest.

The complexity of the underwater terrain around Hawai'i may surpass that of even its most intricate land forms, and the movement of fish through and above the convoluted offshore mountains and valleys is probably best known to fishermen. Although many never see the depths with physical eyes, the mind's eye works hard to know it well—perhaps in a manner similar to Culliney (1988), who describes its variability and splendor in *A Far Sea* (pp. 59–60):

> Another view . . . is achieved . . . in such places as South Kona off the Big Island. Shelving reefs are absent along most of this coast, and right from the shoreline the seafloor descends steadily towards the abyss. . . . The ceiling of fractured sunlight seems very remote . . . the terrain drops away into twilight and then perpetual night, and one can conjure an explorer's image of the inverted Himalaya that lies so near

Swells of southern hemisphere origin breaking near Kupikipikio

> and extends so far. . . . Off some of the older shores of the Hawaiian Islands, modest shelves often a mile or two in width have been built. . . . Such a shelf extends from O'ahu's western coast. In most places it is a composite of two or three terraces descending in wide irregular steps to the edge of the deep island slope. . . . Flanking the major canyons are rocky ridges projecting seaward. These are traceable to the land, where they form the stark, basaltic headlands separating the spectacular valleys incised into the Waianae shield.

Although the ocean around Hawai'i is not, in a relative sense, extremely rich in endemic marine life, it *is* attractive to migrating pelagic fish. It has therefore developed a reputation for good a'u and 'ahi fishing, and many fishermen here have inherited and/or developed a keen understanding of where these fish will be feeding and when, and customary strategies to catch them. As discussed in some depth further along in this case study, knowledge and strategy come from experience and tradition and the interaction of those two, with varied levels of success.

But the Pacific Ocean can challenge even the most seasoned mariner. In winter, North Pacific storm systems propagate deep ground swells that eventually reach island waters. A typical winter swell will initially show from the west or northwest, being generated well to the west and north of Hawai'i, then turn more northerly, and finally northeasterly as the storm moves east toward North America. Meanwhile, the ocean surrounding Hawai'i is churned by predominant east-northeast trade winds. The combination of ground swell, wind swell, and

Winter swells viewed from offering platform above Waimea Bay

directional mixes thereof test the navigational skills and, sometimes, the fortitude of fishermen. Many lives have been lost pursuing fish in Hawai'i.

There are other environmental challenges, too. Some argue, for instance, that the health of fish resources around Hawai'i is suffering from a variety of problems, including diminishing quality of habitat in areas accessible to the small-vessel fisherman. Urban and agricultural runoff, other sources of pollution, and siltation of fish nursery areas are often blamed for this problem. Others blame overfishing and associated mortality of juvenile fish for problems with the resources.

In any case, the status of fish resources in the region has changed since the early twentieth century. Shomura (1987) notes that between 1900 and 1986, harvest of reef-loving fish species in Hawai'i had declined by 80 percent, and harvest of netri-pelagic species such as 'ōpelu (*Decapterus maruadsi*) and akule (*Trachiurops crumenophthalmus*) had declined by 40 percent, indicative of intense fishing pressure resulting from increased human populations and improved fishing technology. Historic figures regarding harvest of pelagic species are hard to come by and thus, gauging change in those stocks is also difficult. These are just a few of many issues that challenge managers of pelagic fish resources in the Central and Western Pacific. Effective management of migratory species is a complex and challenging task that has to accommodate both human and physical environmental factors. But in most cases, science is just beginning to shed light on the pelagic resource, the nature and effect of its pursuit by Pacific fleets, and the physical environment in which it exists.

THE PELAGIC SPECIES

This case study is focused on the small-boat fishing fleet in Hawaii, most participants of which are primarily involved in the pursuit of pelagic species. At least 14 pelagic fishes are pursued in the Central and Western Pacific (see

The prized 'ahi or yellowfin tuna

TABLE 2.1 PELAGIC SPECIES LANDED IN HAWAI'I

Hawaiian	Japanese	English/Scientific	Description
'Ahi	Kiwada maguro	Yellowfin Tuna *Thunnus albacares*	Prized by all fleets, high value
Aku	Mebachi shibi	Skipjack Tuna *Katsuwonus pelamis*	Commonly caught, red meat
Po'onui	Shibi	Bigeye Tuna *Thunnus obesus*	Highest fat content and value
'Ahi pālaha	Tombo	Albacore *Thunnus alalunga*	Relatively low market value
Kawakawa	Suma	Wavyback Skipjack *Euthynnus affinis*	Also called bonito
A'u (ki)	Kurokajiki	Pacific Blue Marlin *Makaira mazara*	Highly prized gamefish; food for Hawaiians
A'u (ki)	Shirokajiki	Black Marlin *Makaira indica*	Dark hue, aggressive
A'u (ki)	Nairagi, Makajiki, Natagi	Striped Marlin *Tetrapturus audax*	Small marlin, high market value
A'u kū	Shutome, Mekajiki	Broadbill Swordfish *Xiphias gladius*	Distant waters
A'u	Hebi	Shortbill Spearfish *Teptrapturus angustirostris*	Sometimes by troll, fighter
A'u lepe	Bashokajiki	Sailfish *Itiophorus platypterus*	Rare in Hawai'i
Ono	Kamasu sawara	Wahoo *Acanthocybium solandri*	Prized, voracious, dangerous on board
Mahimahi	Shiira	Dorado, Dolphinfish *Coryphaena hippurus*	Common food fish, fast, colorful
Opah	—	Moonfish *Lampris regius*	Wandering species, often caught along steep seamounts

Table 2.1). Of these, 'ahi, a'u, ono, and mahimahi are of particular importance to the small-boat fisherman in Hawai'i, to the local and export markets, and to consumers. Significantly, most such species appear to be migratory or highly migratory, passing through parts of the island chain in abundant numbers only during certain seasons.

'Ahi is the most popularly targeted pelagic fish in the Islands. The fatty red meat of the yellowfin tuna is a local favorite, often eaten as sashimi (raw tuna), in sushi, or as poke (pronounced "po-kay"). The latter is a local dish of raw, cubed fish served in a marinade of various ingredients, such as shoyu (soy sauce), green onions, and limu (seaweed). Market prices for 'ahi vary considerably, depending primarily on freshness and fat content. The fish is a voracious fighter when hooked. It can also grow to great size. The all-tackle world record

Local boys with ono and mahimahi

taken off Revillagigedo Islands, Mexico, in 1977, weighed some 388 pounds (International Game Fish Association, IGFA, 1998:218). The Hawai'i state record is 325 pounds. Observation suggests that while fish approaching 200 pounds are not uncommon, most specimens in Hawai'i are less than 150 pounds or so. The fish is native to all warm seas and tends to feed on other pelagic fishes, squid, and crustaceans. Its chief season of capture in Hawai'i is May through August, although this can vary, and it is taken year-round. 'Ahi is the targeted fish at *'Ahi Fever*, the largest fishing tournament on O'ahu, sponsored each June by the Wai'anae Boat Fishing Club.

Po'onui or Pacific big-eye tuna (*Thunnus obesus*) is frequently targeted by ika-shibi (squid-bait tuna) and other offshore hand-line fishermen. The Hawai'i-based longline fleet also pursues big-eye tuna. The fish typically sounds during the day and surfaces at night. This behavior is explained in part by its tendency to tolerate surface temperatures of 62 to 80 degrees but its preference for 64 to 70 degrees (Rizzuto 1987). Because the fish sometimes surfaces during the day, it is occasionally landed by small troll vessels. Young individuals are sometimes found near (relatively) shallow banks. All types feed on various fishes, squids, mollusks, and crustaceans. The fish has a proportionally large head and eye, hence the name in both Hawaiian and English. The all-tackle, world-record big-eye is 435 pounds, caught offshore Cabo Blanco, Peru, in 1957. According to Rizzuto (1987:161), however, the fish rarely exceeds 200 pounds in these waters. The state record Po'onui is 228 pounds. Po'onui tends to produce very high–quality, sashimi-grade meat that is relished by island residents and also exported to the Continent and overseas destinations.

Aku (*Katsuwonus pelamis*), also known as skipjack tuna or bonita, is often caught by fishermen pursuing other pelagic species or is sought as bait for bigger tuna or for marlin. However, some residents relish the fish and sometimes target it exclusively. The aku is said to frequent deep water near the shoreline, especially around the 80 and 100 fathom ledges (Rizzuto 1987:162). It feeds on small fish, squid, and crustaceans in open waters, where it is typically accompanied by terns (*Sterna spp.*) and other seabirds. The birds, in turn, attract fishermen who know that the presence of aku may also mean ʻahi are nearby, or marlin, which feed voraciously on aku. Large visible schools of aku and/or accompanying birds are locally called "piles." Aku was a highly favored fish in ancient Hawaiʻi. Whether this was a result of ease of capture, abundance, taste, cultural significance, or some combination of these attributes is obscured by time. Many modern Native Hawaiians continue to enjoy the fish. It is often cut into fillets, dried, or smoked. According to Goto (1986:93), most aku are caught between May and September. The fish can get quite large, and aku up to 30 pounds are not unheard of in Hawaiʻi. The all-tackle world record is 45 pounds, 4 ounces, taken offshore Baja California, Maxico, in 1996. The state record is 40 pounds, 8 ounces.

Aʻu is the Hawaiian term generally used for the blue, black, and striped marlins, or *Makaira indica, Makaira nigricans,* and *Tetrapturus audax,* respectively. At first capture, the robust-bodied blue marlin is a brilliant cobalt blue along the back and silver along its sides, fading to a slate blue at death. The black marlin can vary in hue but typically is darker than the blue, with a relatively low first dorsal fin and weight carried to the tail. Stripes apparent at time of capture soon fade. The smaller, less robust-bodied striped marlin is royal blue above and silver below, with pale blue stripes and cobalt blue dorsal fins. Longline fishermen in the region report occasional hooking of blue marlin over 1,500 pounds and rare instances of over 2,000 pounds, but there is some apparent dispute about the record catch by rod and reel. IGFA (1998:210) reports that the all-tackle, world-record fish weighed 1,376 pounds. It was taken off Kaʻaiwi Point, Kona, Hawaiʻi, in 1982. Rizzuto (1987:163) and other sources report a fish of 1,805 pounds taken along the Waiʻanae Coast of Oʻahu in 1970.

Hawaiʻi waters, and especially those along the Kona Coast of the Big Island, are known for big blues. While large specimens are desired by many charter fishing patrons and captains who are equipped and experienced for the fight, they are not extremely valuable at market because the meat becomes increasingly tough in fish over about 140 pounds. Large marlins *are* sometimes consumed, however. Some buyers smoke or dry the meat for retail sale, and some local fishermen do so for personal consumption or to share with others. Smaller specimens can sometimes bring a reasonable price at market.

Marlin are not kept or sold in other parts of the United States but are released back into the depths as part of a now-mandatory management strategy and conservation ethic. But many island fishermen continue to eat or sell marlin and question the sensibility of catch-and-release methods. The notion of billfish as "trophies" is also foreign to many local fishermen.

Black marlin also attain immense proportions but are said to rarely exceed 700 pounds or so in Hawaiʻi. The IGFA-recognized all-tackle world record is 1,560 pounds, taken off Cabo Blanco, Peru, in 1953 (IGFA 1998:210). The state-record fish was hooked off Kona in 1980. The fish fought for 12 1/2 hours on 80-pound test line and weighed 1,205 pounds (Hawaiʻi Fishing News 2005). The black marlin feeds on all types of fish and squids and is found across the tropical Pacific. It is reported to be more abundant in Hawai'i during the summer months. A very aggressive fish, it sometimes swallows very large fish whole and occasionally rams boats.

The acrobatic striped marlin, or *Tetrapturus audax,* prefers relatively cool water temperatures of between 68 and 74 degrees and so are most abundant in Hawai'i during the winter months. It often soars out of the water when hooked. According to Squire and Smith (1977:129), the fish averages between 80 and 90 pounds in Hawai'i, with some individuals reaching 150 pounds. The all-tackle world record is 494 pounds, taken off Tutukaka, New Zealand, in 1986 (IGFA 1998:210). The state-record fish weighed 211 pounds. Striped marlin is often the most prized of the marlins and may be sold smoked, as poke, or in steaks.

Ono, wahoo, and the *Pacific kingfish* (*Acanthocybium solandri*) are terms used to describe a narrow, elongated, and powerful pelagic fish with a pointed head and sharp teeth. The dark blue/silver ono is very fast, sometimes reaching speeds up to 50 miles per hour (Rizzuto 1987:175). It often feeds on mālolo (flying fish, or Exocoetidae *spp.*), small 'ahi, and 'ōpelu (mackerel scad, or *Decapterus pinnulatus*) over deep-sea ledges between 25 and 100 fathoms, or near floating logs or rubbish. Ono are dangerous and bite viciously if given a chance. It is also a delicious fish to many Islanders (*ono* means "delicious" in Hawaiian) and brings a good price at market. Ono is particularly tasty grilled or fried in steak form; its round, elongated morphology makes for good steaks. Besides humans, predators include sharks and billfish. The average-sized ono taken here is between 25 and 40 pounds, with larger individuals reaching 60 pounds. The all-tackle world record is 158 pounds, 8 ounces, taken offshore Baja California, Mexico, in 1996; and the state record is 133 pounds, 3 ounces, taken offshore the Big Island in 2000.

Mahimahi is an energetic and voracious feeder and fighter. The Hawaiian term is now often used on the continent as well, but it is also called dolphin, or dolphinfish (*Coryphaena hippurus*). It is sometimes referred to as "dorado," but this can also indicate the smaller *Salminus maxillous.* Mahimahi is a colorful tropical and warm-temperate fish, with a dark-green back, apple-green to lemon coloration along its sides, and areas of bright blue spots. The fish is somewhat triangular in shape, with the head as base where the high sail-like dorsal terminates and the narrowing forked tail section as tip. Males, also known as "bulls" are blunt-headed, while the heads of females are more gently sloped. Mahimahi is said to prefer temperatures of between 74 to 76 degrees, making it most common in Hawai'i in the spring and fall months. Adults like the open ocean but also frequent nearshore waters and are often found in association with floating objects. Juvenile individuals tend to feed on copepods, while adults feed on fish, especially mālolo. Humphries (1999) affirms this; his analysis indicates that mahimahi typically consume juvenile pelagic-stage reef fish and squid, and juvenile pelagic species including 'ahi and billfish. Very large specimens may reach 70 pounds in Hawai'i, with a more typical range between 15 and 25 pounds. The all-tackle world record is 87 pounds, taken in Papagallo Gulf, Costa Rica, in 1976. The state record is 82 pounds.

SMALL-BOAT FISHING GROUNDS AND GEAR TENDENCIES

Having grown up around the very flat coastal wetlands of the Mid-Atlantic and Southeast United States, I am awed by the seismic and volcanic mountain landscapes characteristic of coastal zones in other parts of the country. For instance, compared to O'ahu's Wai'anae Range, which soars straight up from the Pacific, the ancient and heavily eroded Appalachian Mountains, which begin some 300 miles inland from the coast in Western North Carolina, appear as gentle hills. The offshore waters of Hawai'i are also quite different. For instance, the ocean offshore Cape Hatteras, North Carolina, is quite deep relative to other East Coast ports, with the 1000-fathom isobath occurring out past 35 miles or so from shore. But in various places in Hawai'i, the same depth is achieved within a mere mile from the shoreline! This is highly significant for island fishermen, who in many places in Hawai'i catch pelagic species along the 40- and 100-fathom contours, in some places less than a half mile from shore. In contrast, captains pursuing pelagic species along the East Coast must often travel many scores of miles to reach the deep blue water that is the preferred feeding grounds of tuna and billfish. In short, the deep nearshore waters that surround the Hawaiian Islands are ideal for the operation of small boats and captains who prefer fishing for pelagic species.

The small fishing boat is a fixture across the Hawaiian Islands. It can be seen rolling on trailers on the highway in Honolulu, on bumpy South Point Road near Ka Lae, and on little Pu'u ka pele Avenue on Moloka'i. Small boats are moored in harbors across the Islands: at Mā'alaea Harbor on Maui, Nāwiliwili on Kaua'i, and Kaumalapau on Lāna'i. They ply the waters from Punalu'u to Nā Pali, from nearshore reef to offshore buoy, and, on occasion, across the dangerous channels between the islands. Some small-boat captains go after bottom-feeding fishes like ulua (*Caranx ignobilis* or Giant Trevally) and onaga (*Etelis coruscans* or 'ula'ula), and many use their boats as mobile platforms to spear various reef fish species or octopus (*Octopus cynea* or tako) near the shoreline. But almost everybody is rigged to troll (use surface lures at speed). Indeed, even when people use other gear types, they will often troll for ono, 'ahi, and other pelagics en route to their favorite dive or bottom-fishing grounds. Trolling for pelagic species is undoubtedly the most popular form of boat fishing in the Islands and the primary operational and resource focus of this case study.

SMALL BOATS AND GEAR DEFINED AND DESCRIBED

The small trolling vessel can be thought of as the "little guy" of Hawaiian boat fishing. But it is also the most popular. At least 10,000 small boats were operating as fishing vessels around the Hawaiian Islands at the time the fieldwork was conducted for this case study. "Small" in this context generally refers to trailered and moored noncharter fishing vessels in the range of between 16 and 32 feet in length, and up to about 6 to 9 feet in beam. The average charter boat is, by contrast, between about 32 and 45 feet in length (Hamilton 1998), and between 8 and 12 feet in beam—too big to transport by trailer on a regular basis. Longline vessels average about 70 feet in length (Hamilton et al. 1997:4) and 22 feet or so in beam, while the longest aku boat is up to about 65 feet in length and around 20 feet in beam.

Most small troll vessels have an average offshore range of not much more than 40 miles. Captains can go farther with extra fuel cans or reserve tanks, but this is fairly unusual. The mean maximum distance from shore reached by the captains surveyed during the small-boat study was just over 18 miles. Some make interisland passages, and a few will travel offshore in specially rigged vessels and with patently for-profit motives to fish far offshore the Big Island at Cross Seamount, weather buoys, or other distant locations. But the majority of captains engage in trolling relatively close to shore with highly varied, mixed, often overlapping, and situation-based motives relating to economic return, subsistence, enjoyment, competition, and self-identification as fishermen.

Pelagic species feed in the upper levels of the water column. This means that troll vessel captains and crew pursue them by dragging lures or bait attached to multiple monofilament lines via rods and reels. This is the most common way to fish from small boats. Normal troll speed is about 7 or 8 knots. Small lures and hooks are used for smaller fish such as aku, while bigger hooks and lures are used for larger ‘ahi and a‘u. More lines in the water mean better chances for success, of course, and so multiple lines are staggered to prevent tangling. Most captains surveyed report using 5 rods and reels at a time. Some lines are attached to outriggers—long fiberglass poles rigged at angles to the vessel. These also help keep lines apart.

The quality of fishing gear has come a long way in the last 75 years, but the basic technology remains relatively simple: The rod allows the angler to sense biting fish and absorbs the shock of fish that are hooked. Obviously, the reel distributes the baited line through the rod eyes and gathers it back in to bring the fish to the boat. When a fish hits one of the lures on a line attached to an outrigger, the rubber band that attaches fishing line to outrigger line will break, whereupon the torque force on the outrigger line is transferred to the fishing line and rod tip. Some fishermen use a metal clip mechanism rather than a rubber band for this purpose. The hand line typically used in addition to rods and reels on a trolling vessel, and sometimes by itself, is simplistic, typically consisting of a piece of surgical tubing that acts as shock cord, a long nylon line, and a leader rigged with swivel, clip, and lure or baited hook. Both large and small fish can be pulled in by hand, but this requires additional strength and skill on the part of the fisherman to keep the line tight. Otherwise, the fish can work itself loose. Whether trolling or handlining, tight lines are always critical to success. Large, sturdy gear such as the 14/0 or 130 Class two-speed gold reels is used for large fish such as big ‘ahi and marlin, while smaller gear such as the 6/0 or spinning reels is used for aku and other small fish. Most boats have an area dedicated to the storage of various leader material, hooks, lures, clips, and swivels.

Some fishermen inherit gear from their forbears and maintain aging equipment while others constantly trade, resell, and buy the range of new "high-tech" rods, reels, lures, and associated gadgetry. The flea market and swap meets held around the islands are good places to find used gear. In many parts of the Islands, large franchise stores have begun to compete with the traditional small gear

Commercial troll gear in use offshore O'ahu

suppliers. Some fishermen bemoan this trend and fear the loss of relationships with highly knowledgeable salespersons at the latter. Others claim to appreciate the cheaper prices offered at the chain stores.

Small-vessel fishermen normally take good care of their gear because it is expensive and because proper maintenance assures good performance at task. Post-trip duties invariably involve rinsing to minimize corrosion. Many fishermen install rod holders on their pick-up trucks for safe and easy transport of equipment, though some leave rods and reels on moored vessels if these can be secured under lock and key. Conventional model heavy-duty boat rods were running at a minimum of $180 each in Hawai'i during the year 2000, while the average cost for standard 14/0 reels suitable for landing large fish were nearly $400. More extravagant rod-and-reel combinations approached $1,500 each. Standard 15′6″ outriggers started at $245 a pair. With extensions added to create a 25′6″ outrigger, the cost was about $420 per pair. Additional rigging and essentials, such as gaffs, bats, coolers, and other gear, add to operational costs.

Trolling lures vary widely, but size and design obviously relate to function. A savvy captain can determine the size of fish pursuing his lines by visual reconnaissance and/or by the manner in which fish take the lures. Thus, gear and lure changes are common during the course of a given trip. A cadre of expert lure makers now exists in the Islands. Some have developed better reputations than others and so have assumed loyalty among fishermen. Some fishermen make their own lures in garages and shops around the Islands.

A learning curve is associated with use of trolling gear. It is not steep, but basic experiential knowledge can be acquired only after numerous trips, and not knowing how to fish appropriately is something beginners often get chided for (until the novice becomes adept). There are many points at which basic knowledge is helpful and assures safety. For instance, lines must be let out from the reel with thumb or fingers applying friction in order to slow release and prevent tangling. But there is always danger around the lines because a loop can tend to grab appendages, particularly if something takes the line in a hurry, as do big fish. Hooks and gaffs present obvious dangers, and the wise captain will ensure that his crew and guests are well aware of the liabilities. Fish can be dangerous too, as many captains will attest.

Bottom fishing along the nearshore areas may often be a productive venture, but the fish are smaller than those pursued by trolling; the effort requires more directed focus on the part of the angler in that hands are always on rod and reel, and there are no guarantees for success here either. Trolling can be done with minimal hands-on involvement on the part of captain and crew. Once the lines are out, the mission is one of locating fish. Lines may tangle on occasion, but this is easily fixed. Catching large fish on multiple lines during a "rush" is a rarity but can occur and makes for some rich stories. Some captains carry small spinning or bottom gear for optional use if trolling is not productive or if seas limit activity to nearshore areas. Other also carry dive and spear gear on board for optional use. Bottom fishing typically involves use of weighted lines with multiple leaders and baited hooks. The captain drifts over spots that are known to be productive, as the bait or lures are "jigged" near or along the bottom.

Baited hand line methods such as ika-shibi or specially rigged "chum" bags known as palu ʻahi are used while slowly drifting. Though some fishermen have used these and related methods with great (and at times, highly lucrative) success in years past, they are typically used by vessels involved in highly focused fisheries at specific times and places and are not normally used by the average troll vessel. Ika-shibi methods were developed by Okinawan squid fishermen, who realized that by employing a special hook, they could catch the tuna that often made off with the squid as these were being brought to the surface. The method has been developed as a nighttime fishery wherein underwater lights are rigged to attract microorganisms, which then attract squid and ultimately shibi (tuna) to the boat. Many Big Island residents now use ʻōpelu rather than squid to bait the hook. Participation in the ika-shibi fishery has declined steadily in recent years. Palu ʻahi is an ancient Hawaiian method. A bag of palu or chum (shredded or mashed bait) enveloping a baited hook and tied with a quick-release knot is lowered to the depths during the day. When the line is pulled, the bag opens and the chum is released, attracting fish to the baited hook.

Live baiting is used frequently by certain captains. This method typically involves threading small aku, or perhaps ʻōpelu, on a special bridle with hook. Live aku are trolled at slow speeds, while other baits are deployed while drifting. Slow trolling and drifting allow bait to be presented in an appropriate manner while also conserving fuel.

Clearly, there are many gear requirements and options for the typical trolling operation. The fishing vessel itself must also be purchased, and if it is not moored in a specific location, a trailer and a truck of sufficient power to tow the trailer must be acquired. A four-wheel-drive truck is essential in many of the rural areas. Communications and other electronic equipment are also needed or desired. Moreover, each trip requires fuel, ice, food, and drink, and sometimes bait. Hamilton and Huffman (1997:35) reported an average trip cost in the mid-1990s of $134 for boats between 16 and 30 feet, with annual fixed costs for this vessel class approaching $7,000. The costs of fishing are high for some but typically are readily paid to maintain the opportunity to fish.

FOCAL POINTS FOR FISHERMEN

The difficulties of simultaneously navigating the boat and fishing generally call for more than two hands. At least one mate is the norm, but two or more assistants are not uncommon. As such, there is an inherently social element to fishing. There are exceptions, of course, as described in my observations at Ka Lae, and some captains prefer to fish alone. This can elevate their status among peers. Mr. Funaka (pseudonym), for instance, operates a 26-foot vessel on the windward side of Ka'u District on Hawai'i Island. He is over 70 years of age but operates solo and on a regular basis in some of the roughest seas in the Islands. Other fishermen in the area speak of him with great respect.

There is heightened activity and excitement among captains and crew when 'ahi are migrating through the islands. Although timing and place can vary, the 'ahi "bite" tends to be seasonal, with a significant peak in the summer months. As noted throughout, however, big 'ahi and a'u can be elusive, and ono, aku, and mahimahi are more frequently landed.

There is some variability in length of a small-vessel troll trip, depending on the presence or absence of fish, the condition of weather and seas, and many other factors. Survey work revealed a mean of nearly 11 hours per trip, with a modal value of 8 hours, and a range of 4 to 120 hours (N = 150), including time spent preparing for the trip and cleaning up afterwards. Captains fishing purely for profit tend to stay at sea longer, and trips of up to 3 or 4 days are not uncommon. But most captains and crew tend to stay out only for the better part of a day.

Captains often concentrate activities around state-maintained fish aggregating devices (FADs). These were first used on a widespread basis in Hawai'i in 1980 when 26 such devices were deployed around the main islands. FADs of this sort are surface buoys attached to concrete anchors via chain and cable. Sometimes streamers are attached below the buoys to further increase biomass in the water column and thereby attract baitfish and larger predators. Itano (1995:155), citing Buckley et al. (1989), notes that "FADs have been documented by test fisheries to significantly improve catch rates over open water areas, creating easily reached zones with catches more comparable to productive offshore banks and seamounts." The FAD is also very important in a social sense because it serves as a geographic focus for vessel interaction. Some captains began installing and productively fishing private buoys sometime in the 1990s in remote waters offshore Hawai'i Island. This is a story in itself, to be told elsewhere. It should be noted that some fishermen in Hawai'i have resisted establishment of FADs, arguing that the devices divert migrating fish from natural bathymetric features and increase pressure on the pelagic resource.

Trolling for ono along the village Ko'a, Hawai'i Island, 1998

Some veteran small-boat fishermen often like to avoid the crowd and are particularly adept at finding and pursuing the bird "pile." In local vernacular, a *pile* (flock) of birds is indicative of the presence of fish. If those fish are similarly grouped, they also are called a pile (rather than a school). Thus, fishermen might go after a bird pile with the hope of "getting into" a pile of aku. The two are often but not necessarily mutually dependent, however, since a pile of aku, for instance, may be located around a FAD or a log in the absence of birds. Very small groups of birds do not constitute a pile and, unless seen swooping down on the surface, are not considered a reliable sign of fish. But in the absence of other signs, they might be followed in hopes of finding some quarry.

Baitfish congregate around old logs, dead whales, and other floating objects, and so experienced anglers are always on the outlook for these. "Ghost nets" are particularly attractive. These typically are remnants of North Pacific fishing operations with enough floats attached so that some buoyancy remains. Like all objects left in the ocean, the nets become coated with various algae and other marine life, attracting small fish and larger predators. When such items are found, all wise fishermen will thoroughly "work" around the perimeter of them.

A rubbish line is another favored area. This area of floating trash tends to be alternately elongated or compacted by wind and current. As with the buoys, the trash tends to grow various marine organisms that attract fish. The larger the items or grouping, the greater the likelihood that feeding fish will be present, and so what is a plague in an aesthetic sense may be a boon to the fisherman.

The ko'a, or underwater reef mound, is a common fishing spot in nearshore waters, and its location and proper use are often passed on across generations.

Such information is sometimes kept secret, and use rights to such areas are sometimes enforced in various ways by long-time local residents.

Ledges where nearshore reefs drop off into the abyss also are favored spots to fish. For instance, the area around the 40-fathom ledge near one of the Islands is a popular place to prospect for ono.

Finally, colliding currents and thermoclines—areas of significant variability in water temperature—are often sought. Upwelling and mixing of nutrients can occur in such areas, attracting baitfish, predators, and hence, fishermen.

THE INCREASING USE OF ELECTRONICS

Fishermen often communicate to each other remotely by radio, enabling direct communication about the location of fish and birds, fish prices, and other pertinent information. The citizen's band or CB radio is a cheap and effective means of short-distance communication at sea, used to talk from ship to ship and, where range allows and situation demands, ship to shore. The CB was most commonly used by the small-boat fleet in Hawai'i at the time the fieldwork was being conducted for this study. But given advances in cellular and other forms of communication, it is likely a matter of little time before these fully replace the CB. Although it is cheap, the CB is limited in range. The long-range, very high frequency (VHF) radio is required equipment on Coast Guard–documented commercial vessels. It is relatively expensive and was being used by relatively few small-vessel captains I worked with during the late 1990s.

The location of birds and fish is a common topic of conversation among captains at sea, and information can be gleaned through direct conversation with others or merely by listening to the airwaves. The latter may or may not result in reliable clues about where fish are to be found, and in fact, misinformation is sometime broadcast to throw strangers off the trail. When privacy is desired, fishermen will switch channels or use cell phones to converse more discretely.

Most fishermen rely heavily on experiential and gathered social knowledge about oceanographic conditions and fish behavior. Positive reports and the presence of birds and other visual cues remain the primary indicators of feeding pelagic fish. Most captains were navigating by the old methods of compass and landmark triangulation at the time of this study. But global positioning systems (GPSs) are increasingly popular. GPS technology enables fishermen to detect their position on the ocean through electronic-pulse signal interaction with satellites. This is useful for fishing in that it allows determination and recording of distance and direction from one's present location from the harbor and out to the FADs, other vessels, logs, nets, or other areas of reported bird or fish activity.

Use of echolocation equipment (fish-finders) varies across the fleet. Some individuals possess relatively less knowledge of a given area and may come to know bottom contours and underwater features with the aid of echolocation. Captains better versed in local underwater topography may use the devices only on occasion or not at all. When visual cues are absent, fish-finding devices may hold the attention of many captains.

Some small boats are also equipped with autopilot systems. These can be used in conjunction with GPS to plot and automatically direct the vessel's course, leaving the captain free to attend to other tasks with one eye partially on the sea ahead and another on the lines behind!

Communications and navigation equipment are valuable in that they can enhance operations while increasing safety on board. For instance, good communication devices can bring assistance when engines fail, when props get tangled, or when other such problems arise. The rescue of a small troll boat south of Kaua'i in 1999 was originally confounded by lack of a working radio aboard. A long-range VHF radio is particularly useful in this respect. Emergency position-indicating radio beacons (EPIRBs) are invaluable in emergency situations and are required on Coast Guard–documented vessels. Because EPIRBs are costly to some and at the time of this research were not required on the average small vessel, many captains were going without.

FISHING INFRASTRUCTURE

The State of Hawai'i has long been active in providing and maintaining facilities and services in support of its small-boat fleet, thereby enhancing fishing and fishing-related opportunities and related social activities. People meet and interact regularly in the bigger harbors and little launch ramps around the state, and congregate at the offshore buoys and topographic features in the offshore waters. For the purposes of the present research, these were ideal places for observation of fishing-related activities and interaction.

As much as 30 percent of the Main Hawaiian Island coastline is comprised of sea cliffs greater than 30 feet high and 34 percent is comprised of small cliffs less than 30 feet in height (Goto 1986:70). Much of the coastline is therefore inaccessible, except by water. The principal harbors, ramps, and public access points have thus been developed in areas where ocean access and mooring are relatively safe and easily accomplished. For large vessels, leeward shores with deep channels are ideal. Hence, large-vessel facilities have been developed in locations such as Honolulu, Pearl Harbor, and Port Allen. In other areas, such as Nāwiliwili on Kaua'i and Hilo Harbor on the Big Island, manmade structures have been constructed to augment safe passage and mooring. The minimal draft of small vessels allows for easier passage in shallow areas, and so these are the only forms of boat traffic at the little access ramps such as those at Miloli'i and Punalu'u on Hawai'i Island.

The vast majority of small fishing boats are trailered around the Islands. Although this involves some effort and wear and tear on one's truck, there are advantages. For instance, there are no mooring fees, and when word is out about a run of 'ahi, the captain can put in at the ramp closest to the bite. The captain of the moored vessel, meanwhile, might have to navigate significant distances at relatively slow speeds and with considerable fuel cost to get to the "hot spot." On the other hand, the captain who keeps his boat moored can get right on board at any time without going through the hassles of attaching truck to trailer, backing up, finding room to park with a long trailer, and so on.

Some launch ramps and channels are more challenging than others, and many of the most difficult are on the Neighbor Islands (Kaua'i, Maui, Moloka'i, Lāna'i, Hawai'i). Getting the vessel on and off the trailer and in and out of what

Offloading at the steep ramp at Punalu'u, Hawai'i Island

are often narrow channels can be challenging even for seasoned fishermen. An extra hand is useful.

The challenges that can be found at the threshold of land and sea can be considerable in Hawai'i. This was evinced many times over throughout the course of my research. One of the more frightening observations was recorded over Easter weekend 1999, as a small troll vessel entered Hale o Lono Harbor on Moloka'i during a rapidly rising late-spring swell. What had started as a calm morning of light winds and 3-foot seas escalated into a solid 20-foot swell with howling trade winds by midafternoon. The vessel made its way toward the harbor amidst the chaotic collision of trade winds and swell at the harbor entrance. 'Ehu kai (sea spray) filled the air. A slight miscalculation in timing would very likely have resulted in a sunken vessel and loss of life. Although the captain was adept and powered in at the end of a set of large waves, he was nearly pushed into the breakwater as a rogue swell swung in suddenly from the west. But he survived the entry. He subsequently motored into the harbor and set anchor. His complexion was pale and his hands shook as he drove past me in his truck. He stopped for a moment and shook his head, saying only, "Wild, brah (brother)."

TARGETS AND RESULTS

Hana pa'a (hooking a fish) is a most exciting point in any small-vessel fishing trip. Even seasoned veterans may crack a smile when the reel screams. In the ideal case, when the fish is landed it is properly dispatched and iced down immediately. This reduces deterioration of flesh and devaluation at market or table. The size and number of fish landed typically determine whether they are sold or consumed, or both.

Again, 'ahi are particularly valued in Hawai'i. They fight hard, and they are tasty and valuable at the marketplace. Over 56 percent of the 150 captains surveyed during the small-boat fishing project reported pursuing 'ahi on most trips.

Most reported landing aku instead. Mahimahi was reported to be the second most commonly targeted fish, and ʻahi the second most-commonly landed. Marlin was the third most popularly targeted fish; and mahimahi, the third most-commonly landed.

When the trip is over, the fisherman still has much to accomplish. The vessel has to be moored or loaded back onto the trailer and washed down thoroughly to minimize the corrosive (and thus expensive) effects of saltwater on rails, fittings, and other metallic gear. The decks, rods, reels, fish box, and fighting chair are similarly cleaned and rinsed, and the radio and electronics safely stowed. If fish have been caught, they have to be cleaned for consumption or sharing, or prepared for travel to the auction or other point of sale. Ice is a necessity in all cases. Most small-boat captains reported spending about two hours completing various post-trip duties.

The particulars of most trips are recounted on land, though reticence is common in cases where the effort was nonproductive or when the captain decides that the catch and its location are best kept secret. But observation at any harbor or launch ramp in Hawaiʻi at the end of the day will reveal a wealth of fishing-related conversation between fishermen and others interested in the day's events. Fishermen also tend to call ohana and friends after the day's trip to find out how others did and to communicate their own experience, where and how luck was had or not, and why.

A SMALL BOAT FOR HAWAIʻI

People usually attach lots of meaning to their boat, and oftentimes pride is apparent in its upkeep and performance. Small or large, when on the ocean, the boat is home and refuge. I mean this quite literally. The boat becomes a sort of mobile fortress that cannot be left and that has to be protected at all costs. This is why some fishermen in Hawaiʻi attach ti leaves (*Cordyline fruticosa*) to their boats—not only for good luck in fishing but also in offering and for good luck in returning to port safely. Given its importance, I delve fairly deeply here into the evolution of local small-boat design and local preferences.

Fishing along the shoreline is very popular in Hawaiʻi, but being able to access the offshore waters by boat obviously increases one's options and probability for success in catching large fish. There is great variability in small-boat hull make and type, and engine type and size. Average overall length of vessels among our respondents was around 21 feet, with a range between 14 and 45 feet. Some 68 percent of vessels employed one engine, and nearly 30 percent used two. The mean age of vessel was nearly 12 years, with a range between brand-new and 45 years.

The narrow, high-prowed "knife," with attendant sponson (wave/swell deflector on forward gunwales), is a popular "old-school" vessel among Oʻahu fishermen. It evolved from the traditional sampan design brought from Japan during the early 1900s. Its moderate length (often in the 21- to 26-foot range) and relatively narrow beam (width) make it easy to trailer and well suited for speedy travel to and from the fishing grounds. Its tendency to rock in seas is a drawback, but it remains a favorite of local fishermen nonetheless.

But there is a wide range of vessels active in Hawaiian waters. Some are made locally, others on the Continent. There are very old vessels still on the water, as well as brand-new models like the roll-resistant twin-hull said by some (salespersons) to be the new wave of future design. There is a mix of inboard and outboard power, and diesel, two-stroke, and four-stroke engines. Some vessels are suitable for trailering, while others are more suitable for mooring. There are 13-foot boats and brave souls who make the offshore trip to ‘ahi or marlin grounds in good and moderate conditions, and there are beamy 30-foot boats whose unconcerned captains and crew are barely affected even on fairly rough days.

Certain factors bear on the preferred shape and size of the small pelagic vessel in Hawai‘i. First, walking, standing, or sitting on a boat at sea invariably requires holding on, not only with hands but also with the force of leg muscles, feet, and at times, elbows, hips, knees, or whatever is available to help maintain balance. This can make for sore muscles the following day if one is not used to the experience. Thus, there is always some consideration of stability when choosing a vessel. Narrow vessel designs may be faster than beamier designs, but they are less stable in seas.

Second, trailering favors the smaller vessel. Many fishermen undoubtedly curse the choice of a large trailered vessel as they chug up a steep pu‘u (hill), brake for a downhill traffic light, pay for gas at the convenient mart, or struggle with the ball hitch or heavy boat at the launch ramp.

Third, although deep water is never very far from the shoreline in Hawai‘i, this does not necessarily ensure a short trip, as depending on the nature of the bite, prime fishing grounds may be a considerable distance offshore. Even on leeward sides of the Islands, winds and seas tend to increase in proportion with distance from land. Thus, the longer boat and/or the beamier boat that is more stable in seas can be an advantage. The need to cover distance in seas also favors the highly powered vessel and the vessel that burns fuel efficiently. While these attributes can tend toward contradiction, a combination of factors may be desirable to any given fisherman and his preferred style and needs. For instance, while a large boat does well in seas, it is a poor choice for pulling behind a truck, thereby pushing the ideal toward a moderate-sized vessel that works moderately well in seas and relatively more efficiently on a trailer.

Another dimension also influences vessel design: *manageability at task*. The larger the vessel, the greater is the need for crew to assist the captain. If one does not have network of social relations from which to select crew, a smaller, more manageable vessel may be more practical.

The beam size of vessels can also be considered in functional terms. While a wide boat makes for a stable and roomy platform, it reduces vessel speed. Similarly, hull design is a mix of positive and detrimental function, depending on task. A deep-vee hull (a hull shaped in the form of the letter “v” when viewed from the bow) like that of local design helps to cut through seas at speed but results in rocking when not at plane (the speed at which a vessel levels off, thereby reducing drag). A semi-vee hull allows for more stability at lower rpms.The design may also reflect need for comfort. For instance, some fishermen may need a full cabin to enable overnight trips or to shelter the crew from the sun during day trips if so desired. Others may be willing to brave the elements and forego a cabin. Variation abounds. Hamilton and Huffman (1997:39) reported an average vessel purchase price of around $27,604 in the mid-1990s, with mean trailer purchase price at $2,023.

The power source is also a highly variable factor for such small fishing vessels. While few avid fishermen would deny the "beauty" of the quality inboard diesel and its round-the-clock hum of efficiency and reliability, these are not always affordable, nor suitable for every vessel. Generally speaking, the type and horsepower of the vessel's engine are chosen to match the weight and design of the hull. But it can be said with confidence that in the ocean around Hawai'i, where strong currents, winds, and high seas are typical conditions, outboard engines ideally are accompanied by a twin. If and when one breaks down, the other is there in reserve. Of course, the ability to afford a second engine depends on the state of the fisherman's bank account.

Relatively recent advances in engine technology are reportedly having an effect on the small-vessel fishing enterprise and on the boat sales industry. The four-stroke engine has achieved great popularity in Hawai'i, ostensibly for its economy of fuel use, creating a highly competitive environment for the historically popular two-cycle motors. The general formula for the base price of quality

Local style hull with twin engines, Hawai'i Island, 1999

Tried and true wa'a pā still in use at the turn of this century

four-stroke engines is horsepower multiplied by $100. Thus, the popular 115 hp was about $11,500 in the year 2000; the 130 hp, about $13,000.

Of interest with regard to the social and economic dimensions of vessel variability is tradition of vessel use. Certain vessels may go through a series of owners. These often are relatives in the same 'ohana (family), from aging kupuna to son or grandson, from uncle to nephew, from brother to brother's son, from kupuna to close friend. Sometimes the vessel is inherited, sometimes sold, sometimes traded, depending on the nature of the relationship and value of vessel. Many local vessels make the rounds in social circles, and their virtues, true or exaggerated, are extolled in the process. Not everyone is in the market for a new boat, and as the old ones recirculate, their legendary feats and the reputation of their design can grow. For marketers of new vessels, this is a somewhat bothersome phenomenon. A leading boat distribution representative sadly related that the biggest competitor was the used boat of local design. "They go 'round and 'round," she said with a grimace.

One aspect of vessel recirculation is the changing needs of fishermen as they proceed through life. For the sake of manageability in learning and cost, most fishermen start off with a small boat. But as knowledge, fishing relations, and capital accumulate, a bigger and faster boat can be crewed and operated, leading to better opportunities to catch fish and acquire the rewards that can entail. When the twilight years come, the elderly fisherman may have trouble finding crew to assist him. His friends may be fewer in number, and his sons and grandsons may now have their own vessels. It is time again for a smaller vessel that can be managed more easily. This was the case for Kelaula, an elderly man who fishes along the Wai'anae Coast of O'ahu. When his son moved away, he was forced to find a smaller boat easy for him to get in and out of the water.

Fishermen in Hawai'i can often be seen working on their boats. The interaction of engines and vessel with the marine environment invariably challenges one's maintenance skills. Major problems with the engine or transmission may require a lengthy period of nonuse until the problem can be fixed or enough money earned to afford service. Richard, a local Portuguese fisherman living on O'ahu, constantly works on his boat. There is always something wrong and he is always fixing it, often begrudgingly. His fingernails are perennially full of engine grease, and his clothes soiled with fiberglass resin and dust. He curses at the boat, the engine, the tools. But he keeps the rig running and he's a good fisherman. This is a typical case. The more affluent tend to have the vessel serviced, but this is not an option for many.

Some fishermen along the South and Central Kona Coasts on the Big Island still use the wa'a pā, or three-board canoe. This modern version of the ancient outrigger is now fitted with a small outboard engine and is an effective and cost efficient means to get out to the ko'a and other fishing spots along this part of Hawai'i Island.

SOCIODEMOGRAPHIC ASPECTS OF PARTICIPATION

There are similarities in fishing strategies between anglers in all islands and oceans. After all, the process itself is not extremely complex in technological terms. But local knowledge about the resource, the physical environment in which it feeds and migrates, and the linkages between these and other local factors do indeed vary across time and space. Seasoned fishermen in Hawai'i possess great knowledge of reefs and seamounts, interisland currents and thermoclines, the effects of the moon, swell and trade wind interactions, behaviors and interactions of pelagic species with these factors, and other localized phenomena.

A person can, of course, learn how to troll properly through trial and error or by reading how-to books. But it is often the case that the finer nuances of fishing are learned in an extended-family setting or through friends. In Hawai'i, the extended nature of the 'ohana can provide a large set of fishing tutors. Fishing knowledge is vast, important, and, in many instances here, it is communicated across generations in the family setting.

Small-boat fishing in Hawai'i is almost always a cooperative venture, both in terms of specific trips and as an activity over the long term. Relatively few captains fish alone, and even for those who do, there is usually some sort of external support. The involvement of friends in fishing ventures is very important, though in Hawai'i the distinction between friend and family member is less clear than elsewhere.

Some distinctions may be made between commercially oriented operations and those that are more *ad hoc* in nature. Informal agreements tend to keep deck hands true to promises to fish commercially, but high turnover rates and intervessel mobility among crew are common. Operations that are less commercially oriented tend to involve family and friends as crew, and more flexible arrangements. In this case, captains may scold crew who fail to show up in the morning, but there is no "job" to lose.

Males of all ages participate in small-boat fisheries in Hawai'i. Because there are no license restrictions or testing programs, anyone can operate a boat. I observed kids as young as 16 years captaining boats far out at sea during the course of this research. The youngest captain participating in the survey was 18 years of age. The oldest was 75 years of age. The mean reported age of captains was 43 years, with a standard deviation of 12 years.

Small-boat fishermen in Hawai'i tend to be relatively experienced. Survey respondents reported an average of almost 18 years of pelagic fishing experience. The most seasoned reported 58 years of experience. Extensive involvement in commercial fishing was also noted; captains reported having fished on a commercial basis for almost 7 years on average. This is based on reports about how long one has been selling some part of his catch and not (necessarily) how long one has fished only for profit.

Few females participate directly in Hawai'i's small-vessel troll fishery, or did so around the turn of the twenty-first century. Of the many hundreds of operations observed during the course of this study, I observed perhaps a score of women on board small fishing vessels. None of those seen fishing were captaining the vessel. This situation is discussed in later chapters.

Women *do* participate extensively in land-based roles, such as transport of fish to the auction, purchase of ice, paperwork, and so forth. The most commonly undertaken indirect role by persons other than captain and crew was transportation of fish to point of sale. This is a particularly helpful task in that it frees the captain to tend to the boat and associated post-trip duties while expediting arrival at the auction or other place of sale.

SHARING, KEEPING, AND SELLING FISH

An interest in understanding ethnic dimensions of catch disposition and suspicions that rates of selling, keeping, and sharing catch could vary by ethnicity led me to conduct some statistical analysis to test this possibility. But I found no significant differences between ethnic groups in terms of sharing fish (where *alpha* = .05). Sharing some part of the catch appears to be a common aspect of small-boat fishing culture in Hawaii. Intergroup differences approached but did not reach significance for rates of catch kept, where local Filipino fishermen kept 66 percent of catch, local Japanese fishermen kept 53 percent, local Caucasians 46 percent, Hawaiians/Part-Hawaiians 37 percent, and local Portuguese 31 percent. I did find a statistically significant difference in mean rates of sharing between vessel captains resident on (1) O'ahu, and (2) Hawai'i Island. The average percentage of catch that was kept for sharing for residents of Hawai'i was 62.3 percent, while on O'ahu it was 52.6 percent, which for these data is marginally statistically significant ($p = .058$).

I also did some regression analysis with the survey data to explore relationships between keeping, selling, and sharing fish on one hand, and various investment and social factors on the other. Analysis revealed that keeping fish tends to be associated with increasing age, operating smaller boats, and fishing relatively infrequently. Selling fish appears to be related to being relatively young, operating longer boats, and fishing more often. I also found that the number of times a person was given fish during the past week was significantly (and intuitively) related to percentage of catch that is shared ($p = .032$, *beta* = .19). Moreover, an inverse relationship was detected between tendency to fish for ceremonial purposes and percentage of catch sold. That is, fishermen who reported fishing for ceremonial purposes, such as baby lū'aus, weddings, and so forth, tended to report keeping their catch more often, while fishermen who made fewer ceremonial trips tended to regularly sell their catch.

It appears, then, that fishermen in Hawai'i can be logically conceived as participating in small-boat fishing in two general ways. There are always exceptions and the boundaries of the categories are flexible, but observation suggests these are useful and valid ways of thinking about the fishery. One involves relatively older fishermen who are deeply involved in social networks in which fishing primarily for consumptive and ceremonial purposes is normative. The other involves relatively younger fishermen who tend to be more deeply invested in commercial fishing and who mobilize resources with the primary intent of increasing the potential for recovering costs and generating profit. But in any case, sharing fish is very important in Hawaii, and while it is certainly important to Native Hawaiians and a range of rural residents, it is a common feature of life for many in local society as a whole. This is evinced both through analysis of survey data and through my ongoing observation of local social life in the Islands.

THE FISH AUCTION AND MARKETING ECONOMICS: A ROUGH SKETCH

Hawai'i's seafood distribution system is a complex topic but critical to understanding fishing in Hawai'i. The focus here is on basic socioeconomic aspects of small-boat market issues.

The term *market* is used here to connote the point at which fish are formally transferred from fisherman to buyer for the purpose of monetary compensation. This is differentiated from barter or trade of fish, as historically documented and as observed in various rural areas of Hawai'i throughout the course of this research.

A common venue for sale of fish in Hawai'i is the "auction." On O'ahu, this refers to a specific and still-active Honolulu-based auction; and on Hawai'i Island, it refers to a defunct auction in Hilo, now a private seafood dealer. I refer here mainly to the characteristics of the Honolulu auction vis-à-vis small-boat fleet captains on O'ahu.

Captains or crew members transport or ship their fish to the auction, where it is purchased by local, U.S.-continent–based, or overseas-based buyers or their representatives through a bidding process administered by the auction house. The auction owners take a percentage of the sale for services rendered, usually around 10 percent. Small-boat fishermen typically carry their own fish to the auction on ice in fish bags or coolers, in the bed of a pick-up—be it one's own or that of a family member or friend who has agreed to assist. Cooperation between successful fishermen serves to minimize the cost and effort of carrying fish from distant harbors to Honolulu. One fisherman may transport fish one day, and his friend or relative may do the same the next. In the early morning hours, prospective buyers, now often including quality assessment experts from Japan, surround the displayed fish to judge its quality and make appropriate bids. Bid winners then transport the goods, again on ice, to venues for shipment, processing, retail sale, or preparation for consumption.

When they do sell their catch, small-boat fishermen on Kaua'i and the Kona side of Hawai'i Island tend to sell it directly to local buyers who, in turn, sell to restaurants or retail markets. Alternately, they may sell to restaurant owners directly if that is how the relationship has developed. There is limited sale of fish on Moloka'i, where consumptive-oriented fishing tends to predominate. In some cases, commercial operators on the neighbor islands will ship, or more rarely carry, their fish by boat to the auction house or specific buyers in Honolulu.

Fishermen in Hawai'i are required to have a commercial license to sell fish, but as in all places and times, some individuals circumvent the rules. Some may sell at roadside without a license, at auction through other licensed fishermen, or through the "back door" at restaurants. Small-vessel captains who *do* have a license to sell their catch monitor market prices often, usually as communicated by other fishermen who have recently sold their fish or spoken with others who have. Prices paid for the product continually fluctuate, however, depending on supply and demand, quality of fish, and bidding politics, among other factors. Thus, only the most information-rich and akamai (savvy) fishermen will be likely to have an accurate sense of the going market price at any given moment. The cellular phone now augments transfer of such information. Fishermen typically are not given an immediate assessment of actual value upon arrival at the auction, however, but rather will gain only an approximate sense upon depositing the fish. There is always some degree of uncertainty. The fisherman who does leave his fish for bid is sent a check and receipt in the mail some days after it is actually sold at auction. The demands of fishing and/or working on land, and lack of control over the bidding typically lead to one being absent when the fish goes up for bid.

Because pallets of fish are identified at the auction by vessel of landing, there is some degree of reputation at stake in terms of likelihood that the captain in question took good care of the fish from point of hana pa'a (hook-up) to arrival at the action house. Buyers typically know which fishermen regularly bring in fish that was iced down quickly and otherwise well cared for. Some fishermen claim this is not the main factor of consideration, however—that some degree of favoritism is evident and that efforts of the small-vessel fisherman to properly care for fish go unrecognized. This is perceived to be the case especially when small-vessel captains bring in their fish concurrently with big loads of fish from longline operations. The "big–boat" captains are said to be favored in that the buyers prioritize the large quantities of fish from the big boats and pick among individual pallets brought in by the small vessels later, ultimately driving down prices paid for the latter. Numerous small-boat captains also claim there is some degree of "deal-cutting" between the auction operators and buyers who have

ʻAhi for bid at the now-defunct auction house on Hawaiʻi Island

vested interests in certain longline vessels. But small-boat captains often complain about the auction and market and other aspects of this way of life, and it is difficult to assess the reality of stated dissatisfaction. In any event, after communicating with other fishermen or auction personnel about price, some small-boat fishermen may decide the price is too low and keep the fish, ultimately consuming it or sharing it with others. Other fishermen may seek better prices at a local restaurant or retail store. But undertaking this option reportedly entails risk of being "blackballed," that is, covertly refused equitable treatment at the auction at a later date. Wise fishermen who are auction participants but who occasionally sell fish elsewhere do so as discreetly as possible.

It is often said by small-boat fishermen that the primary buyers have a grip on the Oʻahu market and that the individual fisherman suffers while the middleman gains most of the profit. The same was often said of buyers at the Hilo auction, and some ika-shibi fishermen reported occasionally finding better prices in Honolulu despite shipping costs.

I emphasize that when small-boat captains complain, they do so for a number of reasons, some of which they may not be fully aware of or willing to admit. Fishermen tend to value tradition while maintaining an acute economic rationality in the near term. The bigger picture of what they do and where it is leading economically does not always appear to be their main concern. It is clear to me there are cases of mistreatment at the market and elsewhere but also that the complaints of small-boat fishermen stem in part from the fact that the fixed costs and trip-related expenses for small fishing operations are significant and that the catch often brings minimal returns against that investment. What is often a less than highly productive pelagic resource base and ecosystem doesn't help things. If fish *are* landed, compensation awarded the fisherman, when considered over the long term, does not necessarily cover outlay of time and money. But in reality, this may be as much an indirect effect of the inherent nature of the seafood marketing system in Hawai'i and elsewhere, and public reluctance to specifically and sufficiently compensate the harvester for his efforts as it is favoritism on the part of the auction or its buyers.

In sum, the situation of minimal return against investment obviously means that it is quite hard to succeed at fishing for a living. It also means that it is hard for the part-time angler to go fishing when he has to work at a land-based job in order to keep the boat, gear, electronics, and other operational components running. One way out of the conundrum is to minimize investment, operational complexity, and the need for profit. Those who operate motorized outrigger canoes along the Kona coast often succeed in providing fish for their 'ohana and in some cases sufficient catch for sale. In this case, the relatively limited range of the vessels may be offset by (1) a nearshore ecosystem that appears to be highly productive relative to other locations around the islands, (2) availability of other subsistence foods elsewhere in the area, and (3) an extensive and active network of persons who cooperate in subsistence endeavors and often share and barter seafood and other goods.

The strategy of relatively limited investment may be extended to small vessels with somewhat better range, such as the small open-console vessel with small outboard. But this also seems to require productive fishing grounds in relatively close proximity in order to succeed, as along the Kona Coast of Hawai'i Island. Again, there are long-term consequences in both of these cases, inasmuch as this kind of fishing demands as much or more involvement as any other—time and attention that can't be given to activities suited to economic gain in the competitive and capital-based society that over the course of history has come to predominate in Hawai'i. But I'm getting ahead of myself—more to come on this critical point.

SOCIAL CUSTOMS AND INFORMAL RELATIONSHIPS

Operating a small vessel offshore the Hawaiian Islands is often a dangerous venture. Weather and sea conditions and the process of fishing itself present a variety of hazards, especially for the captain of the small and sometimes relatively minimally equipped troll vessel. Sea and swell conditions are an especially critical factor for fishermen and mariners here. One thing that helps is the degree to which fishermen keep an eye on each other and lend a hand when an emergency arises. This was observed repeatedly during my work in the Islands.

Many fishermen will readily cooperate to tow disabled vessels to safety or to fix the problem on site, even when this means losing time on the fishing grounds. Willingness to assist is widespread and appears to relate partly to a practical sense that the assistance may be reciprocated some day, and partly and, perhaps more commonly, to a kind of moral solidarity at sea: A largely unspoken maritime code appears to call on one's conscience to help others in times of need in a harsh and dangerous environment. The effects of this can be observed in times of emergency when the nearest captain will typically rush to the aid of another without hesitation and without regard for whatever mistake was made, the distressed mariner's background, or any other factor.

Solidarity on the water is also achieved through proper etiquette. The kupuna (elder) or tutu (teacher) often attempts to communicate this to the student. As the student learns, he may become a trusted deckhand, gain some reputation as such, and be asked to fish on other than his own family's boat.

The distance that must be afforded other trolling vessels at sea is of particular importance in the code of etiquette that is observably active across the Islands today. It is often said that novice fishermen do not yet fully recognize the potential danger of crossing in front of or behind other vessels. Proper etiquette calls for a bare-minimum 100-yard buffer zone between all vessel extremities, though more space is demanded by some. Thus, when added to the length of longest line, the nearest trolling vessel should be no closer than about 200 yards. With proper awareness this is reduced somewhat when boats run in parallel course, as around FADs, or in cases where the captains know each other well. Additional room is or should be given to vessels that are "hooked up," since things can get complicated when a fish or multiple fish are careening about. Transgression of this zone usually results in some form of rebuke, strengthened when imposed by more than one vessel captain or crew. A fisherman who has had a line cut or his fishing compromised by a vessel passing too closely will often get on the radio to rebuke the offender and to seek the moral support of other captains witnessing the event. Even in the absence of witnesses, the victim may relate the event to others, and the offense will usually incur collective rebuke by the hui (group of friends). This ultimately leads the transgressor to the realization that rules based on common sense have to be heeded or may lead to unnecessary problems with other fishermen.

The same can hold true for customary ethics about treatment of marine resources. For instance, while violations of commonly expressed ethics regarding the taking of immature ʻahi or other species are hard to observe, fishermen talk about witnessing such events and express ill feelings about the offense and offender within and across their social networks.

Fishing and navigating a boat require various skills and knowledge. The importance of social interaction in acquiring these cannot be overstated. Much learning about fishing in Hawaiʻi is acquired in a family setting. But the role of hoaloha (friendship) is also critical in the life of the typical small-boat fisherman in Hawaiʻi. Interestingly, some relationships may be enacted primarily by radio. One fisherman may come to know another through radio conversations and only later come to recognize the other's boat, or his manner of fishing and personality. What began as a fishing-specific relationship may eventually lead to a more general term of friendship on land.

Kōkua (cooperation) is essential when fish are on the line. When a fish takes the lure or bait, the captain and deckhand must interact closely. For the most seasoned fishermen, this can assume an intimate form of communication between the two. The moment of hana paʻa initiates a period of intense concentration and focus on the task at hand. When interaction is practiced, the process of catching fish can be flowing and graceful, and where problems do occur, previous experience typically leads to quick solutions. Since the captain often concentrates on the vessel's course and speed, and the movement of the hooked fish as seen from his elevated or central position, the mate must focus on keeping the line or lines tight and untangled by reeling in the lines quickly and deftly.

Gaffing a fish that has been brought to the boat also calls for expertise and close cooperation. This must be done carefully so as to avoid losing or damaging the creature and reducing its marketability or edibility. The hooked point of the gaff is ideally inserted through the operculum or gill cover and out through the mouth. If the fish is extraordinarily large, two gaffs might be used, one on either side, and crossed at the handle ends. This requires the work of two people cooperating closely and communicating well, particularly in cases where seas are big and the fish is a fighter.

Small fish are less problematic, of course, but when a big fish is on, the ability of the deckhands to negotiate is critical. In situations where deckhands and/or captains are novices or new to each other, commands are necessarily and inevitably issued by the captain. Because entire schools of fish can be attracted to the lures, it is sometimes the case that multiple fish will strike at once, adding to the confusion. Lines get tangled. Fish get under the boat. Sharks arrive. Captain and deckhands get signals crossed. Visiting anglers get in the way. Some fish are lost. Ideally, most make it to the boat and into the cooler. Speech and actions are particularly critical during hana pa‘a and landing, as these phases often constitute the peak of the experience for captain and crew and determine the success or failure of the trip.

Fishing knowledge and experience are not restricted to pursuit of fish *per se*. In Hawai‘i, as elsewhere, the content of that knowledge also relates to customary aspects of space, tenure, and proper behavior when visiting another area. For instance, in certain areas on Hawai‘i Island, avoidance of trouble traditionally calls for consultation with local fishermen or kupuna before traveling or fishing in the vicinity of a village ko‘a. Indeed, elder fishermen in Hawai‘i report that as late as the 1960s and 1970s, tradition would require that fishermen request permission to fish a bird pile when another captain and crew were already there fishing. Sometimes permission was refused.

THE FISHING CLUB AND TOURNAMENTS

The fishing club is a particularly interesting phenomenon in this analysis in that there is some degree of formality in the relationships between members who are otherwise typically very informal in their approaches to life. But there is also significant variation in the way members approach this more formalized setting. My work involved extensive research-related involvement with a single club rather than numerous clubs. I eventually became secretary and board member of a club on O‘ahu, a process that contributed significantly to this project.

Squire (1976) counted about 12 trolling clubs in Hawai‘i in the mid-1970s, and there were 10 active clubs in 1999 (Hamilton 2000). As I eventually learned, much of what transpired in the club in which I was immersed is similar to that of other clubs around the Islands. Interested readers should refer to Severance

(2001), who provides an excellent description of social and cultural aspects of small-boat fishing clubs and tournaments in Hawai'i.

The fishing club I was involved with was formed in the 1990s by two avid fishermen who, in observing the many local captains fishing and hanging around the harbor on a regular basis, recognized the potential for organizing a fishing hui. Early meetings led to recognition that some sort of formalized system of administration would facilitate smooth conduct of meetings, and so a board of directors was nominated and elected. Payment of nominal dues generated enough funds for weekend pupus (hors d'oeuvres) and get-togethers during holidays.

An important aspect of club activities was the conduct of regular fishing tournaments, one per month, with accumulation of points tallied in anticipation of an annual awards dinner at the end of the year. The tournaments are casual affairs in terms of showing up to fish, but they follow a fairly rigidly enforced set of rules. That is, there is no starting line as in large international tournaments. Rather, "start fishing" occurs at a set time but not a set place. But captains can even start fishing late if they wish, as long as participation is registered via CB radio with "tournament base," which is located in a small building at the harbor. A nominal entry fee goes partly into a jackpot and partly into general and charity funds. Some betting on the side also occurs. An average club tournament at the time of this study involved about 10 boats. A quarterly championship tournament offered trophies to winners, and fishermen accumulated points from all tournament catches. Awards typically included quality rods and reels purchased with proceeds from club events and fundraisers, including the most important and time-consuming tournament, attended by hundreds of captains and crew from across the island.

It can legitimately be said that the fishing tournament is the pinnacle of event-specific social solidarity among small-vessel fishing enthusiasts in Hawai'i. Tournaments are a source of fun, competition, camaraderie, and cultural expression. The big events are also sources for generating monies for donation to various organizations that would benefit from programmatic aid. For instance, one recent beneficiary was an elementary-school fish-farm project. The club I worked with also has a scholarship fund.

Prizes for the bigger small-boat tournament events are significant and numerous, financed through entry fees then as high as $350 and through donations from sponsors such as fishing-gear corporations, boat manufacturing and distribution companies, and beer and soda companies. Two hundred sixty boats entered the club's third annual two-day small-boat tournament, with the big winner taking home $10,000 for a 175-pound 'ahi.

The local tournaments are unlike the big international tournaments, such as that held from Kona, at which pomposity and affluence are so evident. The local tournaments involve smaller boats and a decidedly local and blue-collar Hawai'i flavor. There is plenty of serious fishing but also much fun to be had. Tournaments with which I was associated were held in conjunction with local ho'olauleas (carnivals or community celebrations). Months of preparation allowed for successful delivery of "all kine" local food, music, and entertainment.

The bigger tournaments require extensive planning and effort, and lots of one's spare time. The pressure of striving for a successful event inevitably incurs stress because many of the active organizers work full-time jobs. The strains might be mitigated with more widespread involvement of club members, but the fishing club, like all loosely organized groups, always has a core membership of active workers and a component that contributes relatively less.

But the level of camaraderie and solidarity among and between active club members is formidable. Even though members are characteristically casual in their activities, the organization provides a framework for the outlay of individual energy applied toward collective goals. For many, planning and running the big tournament is valued as a means for encouraging public involvement in the local small-boat fishing lifestyle and for its fundraising potential. There is thus an element of altruism in the actions of those who work regular jobs but put in the extra hours over many months to make the event happen. Such kōkua is also notable during other club activities, such as the recovery of sunken ghost nets along the nearshore reef (these can damage reef ecosystems), and during monthly harbor clean-up efforts.

Monthly meetings bring fishermen together for a chance to pray, eat, drink, and "talk story." Hoaloha is observable. But, as in all organizations, all is not always perfect. Deviation from normative behavior may result in some friction. For instance, a stand-in haole leader who tended to speak in overly belligerent tones to other members eventually incurred collective dissatisfaction. After all, the club was organized for the purpose of having good times. Most of the rebuke was held in check and dissipated over time. This is not a keiki (kids') club but rather one of grown men, many who are war veterans possessing considerable experience and wisdom in group settings. Some degree of competition between this and other fishing clubs is notable, but this too is kept at a friendly level.

One potential rift in "my" club was quickly diminished through mutual appreciation of the democratic process. It was a relatively small issue but speaks to an important social process in which perspectives are expressed not only with vigor but also with acceptance of other views. The issue involved a recurring effort on the part of some club members to allow live baiting in the monthly tournaments. Such members claimed to enjoy and excel at this method, and asserted that drifting saved on gas expenditures. But other club members vehemently rejected the idea of deviating from the club's trolling tradition. As one member put it: "We been wahn !@#$#$% troll club from dah start! . . . Why foah we want go live-bait? . . . No can seet around all day like een wahn bat-tahb!" ["We've been a trolling club from the start. Why would we want to allow live baiting now? It's like sitting around in a bathtub all day!"] When the issue was put to a vote, the trollers won out, and the live-bait advocates silenced themselves, with no apparent hard feelings.

Of interest from a social organizational perspective is the larger social network within which the club is situated. An elderly group of salty Hawaiian fishermen sits around the social circle of the club in both a figurative and literal sense. They are always within earshot of club meetings but don't actively participate unless called in to do so. Uncle Saul may offer pule (prayer before eating) and sometimes comment about this or that issue before or after the meetings, but neither he nor any of his compatriots truly get involved. But club members respect the kupuna, especially Uncle Saul. Uncle, in turn, respects oth-

Sunset at sea, fishing offshore O‘ahu

ers and especially his close fishing friend, who was in a rest home during the research phase of this project. His friend has since passed, with great recognition, including a front-page article in the *Honolulu Advertiser* that described his long life as fishermen, mariner, and guardian of other mariners.

When Uncle Saul speaks, and he invariably speaks in a wise and mellifluous manner, he is listened to. He tells of things he has seen on the ocean, and he communicates his understanding of the best way to interact with others in life. Club members know he has experienced and witnessed a lifetime on the ocean, and so respect him immensely. The core club members and the kupuna are often found at the harbor in the evening, talking story, reviewing the day's events and the possibilities for tomorrow's catch. They continue to form their identities against an island context of fish, fishing, and each other, under soaring green pali (precipitous mountains) on the threshold of the Western Pacific.

3/Holoholo

Having grown up around various East Coast ports and beaches, I think I have a reasonably accurate idea of how most people on the Continent define recreational fishing. Recreational fishing there is generally seen as something that is done for sport and that is quite distinct from the workday and commercial activity. Of course, there are people living in Hawai'i who see recreational fishing as operating the same way in the Islands. Many such persons are transplants. Observation makes clear significant differences in the way locals in Hawai'i go about recreation-oriented fishing. This chapter focuses on what "recreational" fishing is like for Native Hawaiians and local small-boat operators in Hawai'i, and the implications of treating the activity in this way. The Hawaiian term *holoholo* is useful here in that it defines both a dimension of pleasure and something more serious. For instance, the term might be used to indicate fun on the water, as in ho'oholoholo wa'a (to sail canoes). But for some Hawaiians and by extension, some locals, the term is used as a euphemism for fishing of all sorts as it is considered bad luck to discuss fishing *per se* in advance of a trip. Thus, when seen departing for the harbor with fishing gear, one might be asked, "Going holoholo?" or offer without being asked, "We going holoholo!" Hence, even when people refer to fishing by using a word that can connote recreation, they are doing so because it is very important that fish are found, hooked, and landed. Anything that would detract from this outcome, whether it is diminished concentration or sense of purpose, or superstition, is to be avoided.

The case studies presented in this and the following chapters describe three different types of fishing in Hawai'i. The studies are one part of a project that progressed through numerous stages over many months, based on a variety of research methods, including background archival work, survey research, and various interviews and casual interactions with many people.

But the really challenging and informative part of the work was the participant observation phase. Again, it was hard for the fishermen to trust a stranger. No doubt certain questions came to mind: What is he after anyway? How will he use the information? Will this haole boy fall overboard? Clearly, there is some degree of risk in taking a stranger to sea. The unknowns of ocean travel and the uncertain reactions of a stranger to potentially unpleasant situations such as rough sea conditions, heat, and injury probably made them think twice. Perhaps most significantly, I might possibly get in the way of an otherwise potentially successful trip. In the end, doubts were overcome, and I participated in an ongoing series of fishing trips, a few of which are described in the following chapters.

Given my concern for providing insight into the typological range of fishing and related implications in Hawai'i, I included the following studies based on their potential for exemplifying that variation. The studies are by nature somewhat idiosyncratic of specific cases, fishing methods, and personalities, of course, but it should be noted that inasmuch as there are social, technological, and economic constraints and opportunities common to all fishermen in Hawai'i, each case study provides empirical insight into how these factors play out in specific real-time situations on the Central Pacific. Further, each study is colored with empirically descriptive context that at once transcends the individual case and setting at hand and gives additional meaning to it and all others. Psuedonyms, including pseudonyms for boats and most locations, are used to protect the identity of the fishermen.

My ocean background helped me on the trips, though the captains might have felt otherwise at times. My fishing was rusty, and I fumbled on certain occasions; fortunately, the mistakes weren't too serious. I did let an aku get away from a slack line on one occasion, however, and although this particular captain was polite, if it had been a more substantial fish, I am certain I would have been scolded!

As fishing is typically not all about catching fish, punctuated as it is with long periods of waiting, there are plenty of opportunities to observe and listen to natural events and conversations. These are ideal for gathering valid information. There is just no substitute for being present and accepted in the natural setting, and to me, the validity of information so gained is worth that of many surveys.

One methodological consideration that should be mentioned is the somewhat problematic nature of taking good notes on board. I felt a need to take as many detailed field notes as possible because each captain, crew, and vessel were new to me and logistic constraints and uncertainties made it possible that they might be available only on the occasion of the particular trip at hand. At times, the need to concentrate on notes took away from my ability to assist the captain and crew. But I was always ready to put the pen and notebook aside to help out, and this was often the case.

It was also physically difficult to write on board. The constant rolling of the vessel in the swells and seas and the resulting need to hang on required that I sit down while writing, legs fixed to bait box or seat, elbows to gunwale or rail. The wind also made writing difficult, and most notes were taken in small notebooks or on the small quarters of sheets of folded paper held in the palm of one hand to avoid pages blowing around.

Note taking was awkward for another, more cerebral reason as well. There was worry from the start that the process would bother the captains, who might have held the opinion that a visitor should watch the lines astern, the sea ahead, and the sky above, and not write—that the research would be a practical liability or even "bad luck." I asked the captains early on if note taking was okay. They offered universal acceptance and good, if rudimentary, understanding of what I was up to and the potential value of the project.

At the end of one trip, I was responsible for holding the boat off the rocks at the ramp as the captain went to get his truck and trailer. The wind was up, the rocks were slippery, and I was up to my thighs in the water. My notes were in the pocket of my shorts, just above the waterline. A strong gust blew the stern of the vessel, with engine and propeller exposed, quite close to the rocks. Thinking about the health of the vessel and not that of the notes, I quickly jumped in to push off the stern, immediately realizing that immersion might ruin the hard-won notes. I quickly pulled them out and held them with my teeth like a pirate with a knife. Fortunately, they were just a bit wet, the ink blurred in only a couple of spots: a lesson learned in preserving the fieldworker's traditional recording medium.

RECREATIONAL FISHING IN HAWAI'I: A BRIEF HISTORY

It is clear that the ancient Hawaiians enjoyed the ocean. They invented surfing, after all, and it seems fishing and all ocean activities were central to ancient Hawaiian society. Though fishing was essential to survival from early on, at times it clearly had to be enjoyable. Consider the words of Corney (1896) who describes his observations of men catching aku from canoe with barbless hooks; persons who enjoy catching fish might appreciate the scene:

> A canoe that pulls seven paddles goes to sea with two good fishermen (besides the paddlers), each with a stout bamboo [pole], about 20 feet long, and a strong line made from the oorana [olonā] . . . the line is about three-quarters of the length of the pole, and has a pearl hook made fast to it. The canoe is then paddled very swiftly with the hooks touching the surface of the water, one at each side, the fisherm[e]n holding the rod steady against their thigh, and the lower end resting on the bottom of the canoe; they steady the pole with one hand, and, with the other keep throwing water on the hook, and when their prey gets hooked, by lifting the pole upright the fish swings in, and is caught under the left arm and secured. In this manner they will take 40 to 50 in the course of a few hours.

But recreational fishing as popularly conceived on the Continent—that is, fishing *just* for fun and in *opposition* to work on land—has a relatively brief history in Hawai'i. This notion arrived with the European and American haole (foreigner) around the turn of the twentieth century. Generally speaking, fishing as a form of recreation was to be done after the workday was over for the haole middle class, probably in converted sampans (Schug 2002), or by elites who didn't have to work at all. There is not a good record of the extent of this type of fishing in Hawai'i, but it is clear that it may not have registered very well with Native Hawaiians and various recent Asian immigrants who, if they could maintain a boat, were usually fishing in an attempt to make a bit of money or in pursuit of food for purposes of survival.

Major nineteenth-century disruptions to Native Hawaiian society, such as the Great Mahele, meant that any kind of boat fishing that was done was related to subsistence pursuits by an increasingly marginalized people. The Great Mahele was the period between 1848 and 1850, when institution of fee simple rights and transfer of land titles ultimately enabled haoles to purchase land, dispossessing thousands of Hawaiians from their ancestral ahupuaʻa—mountain-bounded valleys within which available resources from mauka (mountain) to makai (sea) were managed and utilized. The importance of subsistence-oriented fishing held true for Native Hawaiians into much of the twentieth century and lingers as we enter the twenty-first. Early twentieth-century immigrant groups such as the Chinese, Filipinos, and Portuguese also had little time or wherewithal to fish from boats on a recreational basis while working the plantation fields all day, day in and day out. Moreover, as described in the following chapter, although some *issei* (first generation) Japanese immigrants were especially good fishermen, theirs tended to be a commercial endeavor.

All manner of small-boat fishing was limited or precluded around the Islands during World War II, but war-related developments in boat design, small engines, and hull materials eventually reached the general public. Hawaiʻi's small-boat fleet grew dramatically with the introduction of fiberglass technology and initial refinement of inboard and outboard engines during the late 1950s and '60s. A study conducted by Hawaiʻi's Fish and Game Division between 1958 and 1961 confirms the increasing popularity of small-boat fishing at the time, with an estimated average of 555,000 annual small-boat fishing trips made along Oʻahu's coastline during that period (Hoffman and Yamauchi 1972:5).

Johnson's introduction of the loop-charged engine in 1968 revolutionized the outboard by providing increased power, efficiency, and especially reliability for the small-vessel fisherman. Marine communications electronics also developed and became more affordable. Modern trolling and the luxuries of increased range and safety thus became accessible to the average fishing enthusiast in Hawaiʻi, and the 1970s were a period of further increases in the number of persons fishing from small boats in the Islands.

All of these changes occurred in tandem with a building boom on Oʻahu and to a lesser extent on the Neighbor Islands. Local wage workers whose parents or grandparents could afford a boat and had established themselves in the plantation economy or in other venues increasingly took to the ocean to fish as a form of activity distinct from their land-based jobs. But from the start, local economic conditions and lingering traditions meant that fishing for food and money was intertwined with recreation. Some of the local Japanese families who were forced to leave the small-boat commercial fishery during World War II probably began fishing again around this time.

As was the predecessor to the fish auction in Hilo, the Hawaiian Tuna Packing Company and the Honolulu Fishing Company were there to buy fish as the small-boat fleet expanded on Oʻahu after the war. The auctions provided easy options for sale of fish by captains active during the small-boat boom, and many people who fished sold to restaurants. Thus, from the start, local small-boat operators were able to recuperate some of the costs associated with fishing by boat, thereby confounding identification of "recreational" activity for much of the local small-boat fleet.

OVERVIEW

As noted earlier and as demonstrated further along in this chapter, not selling fish is not necessarily an ideal definition of recreational fishing in Hawaii. At the least, though, it is an indication of participation in fishing that is *not* commercial. Hamilton and Huffman (1997) report that 28 percent of the nearly 500 small-boat fishery participants responding to their survey reported not selling any portion of their catch. The small-boat survey I worked on indicated the same for about 22 percent of the 150 respondents. Hamilton and Huffman also indicated that the recreation-oriented portion of their sample reported by a significant margin the highest household income, with an annual mean of $68,467. By contrast, the commercial fishing component of their sample reported earning $51,919 on average—perhaps an indication of the effects of that line of work relative to others. My analysis indicates that fishing trips that do not involve sale of fish are typically shorter than those that do, with a mean duration of just under eight hours. These are typically taken about 4 times per month, with a mean of 7 times for retirees.

A "recreational" element runs through all kinds of small-boat fishing to greater and lesser degrees, as it has for centuries. The term in that larger context can mean many different things. I work through some of the complexities of the concept as we move through the subsequent case studies. For instance, one of my more hard-core informants reported perceiving fun in what I decided were some the worst of sea conditions encountered during my work in the Islands. This was a guy who would rather go fishing in a gale than eat for free at the finest seafood restaurant in town. This Native Hawaiian thoroughly enjoys the elements and never has sat nor ever will sit behind a desk wearing hard shoes and a tie:

> Brah, I love when da outreegahs toucheen da trough. You know you leeving den, eh? You got to go rough wah-dah, dat's whey-ah eet's at brah. . . . I love lookeen ahp and see da kine ah-hee cah-meen tru dat beeg blue swell, eh? . . . Den pow, pow, pow—who-kahm ahp brah!
>
> [I love fishing when the seas are so big that the outriggers are touching the trough of the waves as you go up the swell sideways. Then you know you're living, know what I mean? You have to fish rough water, that's where it's at, brother. I love looking up and seeing those tuna coming through the face of those big blue swells. Yes? Then pow, pow, pow—you start hooking them up, brother!]

But most people probably think of something a little more placid when they hear the phrase "recreational fishing." A more casual kind of approach is indicated through some analytical field notes from a trip I took with Drew, a guy who had moved to Hawai'i from the Continent in the late 1970s and stayed. He's devoted to the mainstream work ethic and gets at least 40 hours in behind the hammer rather than the desk, if you will, each and every week. Though his time on the water is limited, he makes the most of it when it comes. There's a Hawaiian-style twist here too, however, in that Drew has a commercial fishing license and will sell his catch if it's good and the prices are right. If it is not, he will usually eat it, and if it is somewhere in the middle, he will share some, too. Drew has been assimilating local culture since arriving, and although he still resists it in some ways, he embraces it in others. His is a decidedly opportunistic and low-key venture, but he loves fishing and it makes his work week tolerable:

> The captain is very busy these days, mostly with one large contract, though he has lots of side work too. He has little free time, but he will get out on the water whenever he gets the chance. Lately this has been about once a week, though over certain parts of the year he may sometimes fish only twice a month and not necessarily on weekends. He says that he moved his business from a location closer to Town so as to be in closer proximity to the harbor and his boat. Thus, when word is out that fish are biting, and if he is free, he can fish, starting even in the afternoon hours. This requires some degree of readiness of vessel, and though he prefers having crew aboard, he will go alone if necessary. Drew makes clear his love for the sense of freedom afforded on the ocean, and its value in relieving work-related stress.
>
> With respect to the idea of selling fish in order to pay for trip expenses, Drew laughs at the notion, asserting what, to him, is the extensive cost of vessel operation and maintenance. According to the captain, even great success couldn't begin to pay for his operation, even at its small scale. Drew estimates expenditures of between $7,000 and $8,000 dollars this year, probably a bad year, but not atypical for any vessel in the 26' range that has some years on it. This includes: vessel dry docking for bottom scraping and painting and associated expenses; harbor mooring fees and electricity bills; prop work; fuel and oil; monofilament line, leaders and lures; a new gaff (lost overboard), engine hoses, fittings, and associated maintenance; new battery; electronics repairs; steering cable replacement; and various upholstery work. "I might as well cash it in and fish [as a patron] on a charter boat," he says, jokingly. He also mentions potential additional costs. A hurricane, for instance, would require that he purchase a trailer to evacuate the boat. Insurance for hull damage, at between $700 and $800 per year, is a considerable expense too, and one he is no longer willing to pay. Fishing for Drew, is, in his words, "mainly for fun."
>
> But the concept of "fun" as it relates to fishing in Drew's case is somewhat loaded with meaning, for fishing is an indispensable factor in defining his life. Subsequent interviews with the captain and observation of his lifestyle reveal a wide range of factors that elaborate the meaning of fishing for fun. The ability to fish to reduce work-related stress and difficulties is certainly valued. While lots of expense and effort are an intrinsic part of fishing, for Drew the hours of relaxation afforded while on the water outweigh these costs.
>
> There are other attractions as well. The captain cites his love for the anticipation and challenge in the chase. He says that one never knows what will happen, and the possibility that an outrigger will take a big hit is ample reward for patience. He also likes competition with his peers and frequently participates in light-hearted wagering and small tournaments. Drew doesn't deny his taste for fresh fish either, and adds this to his list of motives and incentives. He also likes bringing inexperienced people on board and savors watching them experience the "thrill" of hana pa'a. He says, too, that camaraderie is an important reason for his fishing and this is easily evinced by

observing the captain interacting with others. He loves to listen and to talk with other fishermen and does so regularly. His wide smile reveals his friendly nature. While appreciation of camaraderie may be peculiar to Drew's personality and that of other club members, one merely need listen to any CB conversation to realize that socializing is a pervasive and important part of small boat fishing in Hawai'i.

Finally, it's clear that enjoyment of the natural surroundings afforded by boarding a small boat is crucial to the captain's well-being. The construction trade is particularly demanding of body and mind, and the stress of the everyday world of work is released on entering a different environment. Drew reveals this perspective in his own way:

". . . I get my pleasure [fishing]. Yeah, it's a hefty price to pay for freedom, but there's nothing like it. . . . Pau hana (quit work time), let's get a couple beers, head out and watch the sun go down. . . . I'm on instant vacation." (Field notes, 1999)

There are many pleasures to be had on the ocean, including the joy of "getting away from it all," whether "it" be one's job, relationship, the land, or whatever calls for escape or avoidance. Freedom from some relationships notwithstanding, fishing for fun in Hawai'i often involves a strong social dimension, and trips are often taken in part for the purpose of entertaining guests (like me), who tend to be amazed at the beauty of the surroundings.

The first trip described here captures much about what should be distinguished as recreational fishing Hawaiian-style. The participants are intimately involved with fishing, and it is part of their heritage. But it is somehow both central and tangential to their lives, which in daily reality revolve around a mainstream world of land-based work. The family of interest is part of what might be called the Native Hawaiian middle class. They have been deeply involved in fishing and community activities along this stretch of coast for decades. It is the strong local ethos of family involvement that is a defining factor of what is unique about the way they fish and the way other local folks treat them (respectfully). The participants are indeed Native Hawaiian, and this has a deep influence on the nature of this particular trip, this manner of fishing, its history, and the way it plays out in this contemporary setting.

SUMMER TROLLING: HOLOHOLO AND FOOD FOR THE 'OHANA

I met Kimo, captain of *Au Punahele,* in July 1998. My contact knew Kimo well; he had been renting a slip at the harbor for years. The two stood on the pier, joking and talking about the bite or lack thereof as the captain and his son Kaipo worked on the vessel in preparation for a trip the following Monday morning. I was introduced to the long-time fisherman and was told that he started fishing "not long after bone hooks." The captain shook my hand and looked into my eyes, smile widening as he responded quickly and in self-deprecating fashion: "Yeah, but now my hooks rub-bah!" ["Yeah, but now my hooks are rubber and can't catch a thing!"] We talk briefly, and Kimo says he would be glad to take me fishing. I am to meet him at the dock at 6:00 sharp Monday morning.

July 1998 was a month of occasionally brisk trade winds on O‘ahu. But the second week of that month was unusually calm, even into the afternoons when the trades are usually "kicking." It was one such calm, partly cloudy, humid morning that I joined the crew of *Au Punahele* for a day of fishing along a beautiful stretch of Hawai‘i coastline. Again, my geographic description is intentionally vague and obscured to protect the anonymity of the participants in this island context, where local residents know so many other local residents.

The Crew

5:53 a.m. I arrive at the dock a few minutes early but find everyone already aboard and the vessel idling. Captain and crew have already made all preparations, so there is no opportunity to assist. I board while young Kaipo loosens the lines. We immediately back out of the slip, spin around, and head out slowly toward the main channel. There is relatively little activity at the boat ramp this morning. Only four vessels and crews of fishermen are in sight. There is little swell, and passage through the harbor entrance is uneventful. As soon as the jetty is cleared, we begin a slow northwesterly course.

Kimo gives the word almost immediately, a little after six o'clock, and Uncle Bill and Kaipo quickly let out the lines and lures. The center rig, with 130-pound test line, is let out first, to about 70 yards. The sides are similarly rigged but go out to about 85 yards. The outriggers are swung wide, and the port and starboard lines are rigged with rubber bands, ready to snap at hookup. The center line is attached with rubber bands to the lower part of the stern outrigger. The corners are let out last. These are rigged with 80-pound test line that runs directly into the water about 60 yards behind the vessel. The crew works with speed and efficiency. It's clear they've worked together as a team on many previous occasions.

The captain introduces his son, an agile and wiry kid in his mid-teens who competed in an international judo tournament over the past weekend; his wife Leilani, who sits happily on the bench next to her husband in the tower (a fairly unusual instance in which a woman is on board); and Bill, an old salt and friend of the family who later reveals he has many years of experience as deckhand on a variety of vessels in Hawai‘i and along the U.S. East Coast. Everyone is friendly and seemingly glad to have me aboard. Although Kimo already knows, I reiterate my intentions for going along on the trip: to fish with as many folks as possible to gain a direct understanding of the nature of small-boat fishing in Hawai‘i.

Kimo is a schoolteacher, very intelligent, widely read, well traveled, and highly experienced on the ocean. I stand on the main deck near the ladder and lean forward to speak and to listen to him talk story as he navigates the boat on a westerly course. My head is just above floor level a few feet behind the captain's chair. Kimo talks while watching the sea ahead, occasionally turning backwards to talk. At one point during our conversation, the captain suddenly throttles down to idle, gets up, and climbs down the ladder to the main deck. It seems something isn't quite right with the engine, and he hears it. He deftly lifts the hatch to the transmission and reaches down to check the fluid level as Kaipo stands by watching, hands on hips, a frown on his young face. There is not enough fluid, and because Kaipo was in charge of checking engine oil and transmission fluid levels, he gets a somewhat stern lecture on proper reading of the dipstick. Kaipo is respectful and silently takes his medicine from makua kāne (father). Kimo adds some fluid, which is stored below; restores hatch cover; returns to the wheel; and throttles back up. We're off again.

I notice the casual and practical dress of everyone on board. The captain wears loose-fitting shorts and a paint-splattered sleeveless T-shirt that reads "UH–Hawai'i Football" on the back. Leilani wears shorts and a plain T-shirt, and Kaipo wears just shorts. None of the Hawaiians wears footgear. Bill wears a "Gray's Taxidermy" T-shirt, old corduroy surf shorts, and worn slip-on canvas topsiders with socks. He notices me looking at the socks and explains that he had received a mahimahi bite some weeks earlier, that it had become infected, and that the sock was keeping the wound covered.

Au Punahele

Kimo's boat has seen some years but remains a sturdy and reliable craft, heavy by current standards. The captain asserts that, in this case, weight lends stability. I feel similarly about surfboards and understand his rationale. There often is extensive chop and current running up the steep swell faces in Hawai'i, and despite the current trend of smallish, light surfboards, I trust my faithful, old, relatively thick and heavy board. It glides in easily and is unaffected by the chatter. One gets the feeling Kimo would trust his old boat over any shiny new vessel. Kimo's boat has seen many trips and is a little weathered, but he maintains it well and it's ready for action.

Au Punahele is a 28-foot fiberglass craft with about 10 feet of beam, powered by a 653 diesel engine. The midships deck space is an elevated bridge of sorts, where the wheel, throttle, electronics, captain's chair, and bench seat are situated. A bimini (canopy) affords shade. The bridge is accessed from the stern deck space by an angled 5-foot ladder. The deck is roughly 7 feet in length from step-down cabin entrance to transom. The belowdeck area is relatively spacious, with a galley, a head, and various berths. It's full of all sorts of gear and is a bit disorganized. The belowdecks windows are tinted deep blue, and a square Plexiglas hatch cover acts as a skylight for the forward berth. A large fish box is situated along the starboard side just aft of midships, next to the fighting chair, behind and below which are hatches to the engine and transmission.

The captain occasionally makes use of a "green stick," a long, green, outrigger-like pole mounted vertically at the stern end of the bridge. This can be used to drag a winged device known as a "bird" on the surface far behind the vessel. Prospective lure-consuming fish try to outrun the bird, attempting to feed on a series of squid lures that are clipped to the main line just at or slightly above the waterline some distance ahead of the bird. When large fish take a lure or lures, the pressure on the main line is transferred from the green stick to a single rod and reel via a breakaway system, whereupon the angler begins reeling in the fish. Kimo also has the option of attaching the line to an electric winch that, when activated, automatically reels large fish to the boat. The green stick/winch combination is capable of dealing with the largest of fish, bringing them aboard with relative ease. The presence of the rig speaks to the captain's rational desire, and perhaps that of many Hawaiians and other Pacific Islanders I've met, to get big billfish or ʻahi on board, so they can be eaten or shared and/or sold, rather than merely fought and released, as is the trend in some parts of the world. The game of the fight is superfluous, and Kimo offers no apology here; he says, "We like drag 'em right ahp."

Huggeeng Da Ledge

6:35 a.m. We hug the coastline on the way to Ka Lae Loa, fishing the 40-fathom ledge for ono all the while. According to Uncle Bill, our plan is to "fish the ledge, then head up the middle" to the local FADs. There is very little swell, and the ocean surface here is as smooth and fluid as undulating green-blue silk, though it appears a bit choppier farther from land. A large tanker looms on the distant horizon, seemingly making its way from the next island in the chain. Kimo scans the sky for birds and the sea surface for fish while Leilani relaxes on the bench seat. Kaipo listens to the men talk for a moment, then decides to retire to one of the berths, asking Bill to let him know if something happens.

Bill has a vast reserve of fishing tales. He talks story for the next half hour, inciting laughter with each new yarn. He relates the story of a shoreline fisherman who, some years back, handily found a marlin stranded in a tide pool along the shoreline up by the Point. The story is amusing in itself, and Bill's animated style and gestures tickle the audience as he tells of the serendipitous find and of the policeman who called for backup after stopping the angler for speeding and seeing what turned out to be marlin blood dripping from the trunk of the man's car. The stories keep coming until my sides ache from laughing, and I finally realize that stand-up comedy is one of Bill's practiced duties as a deckhand on the vessels he crews. This quality, combined with decades of ocean experience and a calm demeanor, undoubtedly makes Bill a valuable presence on board.

7:35 a.m. Roughly a mile from the Point, under the jagged brown pali of the northern valley, we slowly shift our trajectory westward until we begin to approach an area where trade wind–driven currents and surface waters collide with calmer leeward waters. Even on relatively calm days, this area has an agitated and foreboding look to it. In winter, or during other periods of large swell and strong trade winds, this spot can be difficult to navigate, though it is sometimes considered a likely spot for the bite and attractive in that sense. We turn to the south and east, back toward the ledge. Not long after this shift in direction, I hear Kimo on the CB for the first time, talking to some friends who made a similar directional change earlier in the morning. Their report was that they had tried to fish the area but found it too rough and made for an inside ledge instead. As he talks with his friend, the captain reaches into a small cooler, pulling out a soda and a plastic container of dried 'ahi. Kimo eats and drinks as he steers. Leilani casually reads a book in the early morning light, occasionally dipping into the dried fish herself.

A boat appears in the distance to our south as we near the ledge on our way back from Ka Lae Loa. We eventually pass at relatively close quarters on parallel but opposing courses. Kimo knows the captain, and although there is no radio talk, the two trade hand signals and smiles as they pass within 125 yards or so. Kimo raises both hands off the wheel about 18 inches apart. His gesture asks for the size of the other captain's largest fish. But the reply is a both-palms-up "no moah nah-teeng" [nothing caught], and Kimo indicates his own lack of luck thus far with the same gesture. Another vessel follows about a mile behind in our wake. It seems the ledge is a popular if unproductive course this summer morning, and we head out to the buoys.

8:01 a.m. The trip to the first buoy is uneventful, and upon reaching it, we begin navigating a large circle that takes about ten minutes to complete. But the fish-aggregating device does not seem to be aggregating this morning. After some minutes of heightened attention to fishing and looking for signs of birds and fish, Bill and I resume conversation. He keeps me smiling. Between jokes, he says that during a good year he will fish as many as 320 days per year. This year he's been supplementing fishing-related income with part-time maintenance work at a nursing home. Bill works on four different vessels for pay but fishes with Kimo for fun, as "an old friend of the 'ohana." Kaipo, meanwhile, fishes only with his father but not on every occasion. Bill sometimes fills in when Kaipo is unavailable.

Bill says fishing has been relatively slow during recent years. This precedes a more serious conversation during which the deckhand speaks extensively and seriously about the marine environment and the state of the pelagic resource in Hawai'i. According to Bill, the longline fleet is largely to blame for diminishing resources. His theory is that the longline fleet is hyperefficient and that when each longline vessel's 2,000 or so hooks are strung out along the fringe of the island chain, the result is a "chain-link fence" through which fewer and fewer fish can pass. Bill contrasts this with the small-troll vessel, which fishes with so few hooks. Another of Uncle Bill's concerns includes what he sees as waste through by-catch. He argues, for example, that "they can't use an 800-pound marlin, so over the side it goes," meaning that the longliners generally don't profit from the relatively low prices that large, space-consuming billfish fetch at the market. Although I don't have direct evidence of such actions in hand, such are some of the issues pertinent to fishing and fisheries management in this and other regions of the world's oceans.

No Mo-Ah Nah-Teeng

8:14 a.m. Kimo can hear our conversation about the difficulties of small-vessel trolling and he looks at me occasionally, shaking or nodding his head as his perspective on the issues warrants. Then he looks back at Bill and throws up his hands, signaling his giving up on the buoy. There are no fish here. Bill copies the gesture, adds a frown, and looks at me as if to say, "Another case in point."

Amidst the drone of the engine and the slight rocking of the vessel in the small swell, I ponder the future of marine fisheries in the region. A small pile of birds heads south off the starboard side. Bill remarks that perhaps we're headed in the right direction but that if this effort doesn't pan out, we'll "blame it on the full moon." This stimulates some conversation about factors that lead fishermen

Patches of blue above O'ahu waters during a trip in 1998

to fish or refrain from fishing. Lunar considerations figure prominently in the discussion. Bill also talks about superstitions. One clearly defies economic rationality in that it requires replacing ice between trips to ensure a good catch.

Wahn Feesh Ahn Brah

8:47 a.m. Bill, who is facing the stern and watching the lines, starts suddenly from a previously relaxed position, his eyes widening and mouth forming a look of surprise. He yells over the engine to report a strike to Kimo, whereupon the captain throttles down just slightly. Continued pursuit of birds has finally yielded a strike; the reel doesn't scream, but the port corner line unwinds rapidly from the small reel. A fish is on!

Leilani looks up from her book but remains seated. It's clear that captain and co-pilot have had lots of experience with big fish and already know this is a small one. I grab the rod at Uncle Bill's prodding and begin reeling. Within a minute or so, I lead the fish to the stern. Bill deftly uses the gaff to grab the line before carefully pulling the fish up by hand by the leader. It's an aku, about 4 pounds worth. Bill frees the hook and deposits the creature directly into the fish box as Kimo throttles right back up to seven knots. Leilani returns to her book. Bill says the fish would be the perfect size for marlin bait on a live bait bridle, but this one will be for kaukau (food) tonight. He jokes, saying, "If the fish had stayed in school, he wouldn't be in the trouble he is in today!" Bill says he likes aku because they are easy to locate and hook, and they put up a great fight for their size. He says, "A 20-pounder will make a believer out of you!"

Kimo pilots *Au Punahele* in large circles around the area of the catch, under a small and relatively diffuse pile of birds. Other boats are in the vicinity, but after about 20 minutes, we're alone again. But the bird pile is still somewhat intact, and we stick with the creatures as they glide and drop along a southeasterly course. At 9:20, we have another strike on the same reel! The line departs a bit more vigorously this time as the fish sounds for the bottom, and Bill grabs the reel quickly and begins reeling and pumping. It also is brought back to the boat rapidly—another nice aku, perhaps 6 pounds in weight. Captain and crew remain intent on fishing, but their expressions seem relatively nonplussed. It is as if the catching of aku is expected. Bill shuts the lid on the fish box, and the fish reacts violently with rapid and forceful flaps of the tail. But the captain's attention is focused on the sea ahead, Leilani flips a page of her book, and Kaipo snores in the comfort of the bunk below. Perhaps a marlin would shake things up a bit.

Kimo communicates our catch to another captain, a friend who is presently live-baiting at a distant buoy. He contacts the fisherman on the main channel and then agrees to go down a few channels to talk more discreetly. That fisherman is having limited luck and tells Kimo he is considering meeting us on our journey south and east.

False Alarm: Jah Sahm Rubbeesh

By 10:02 a.m., the bird pile really seems to have fallen apart, and we start heading toward land and the 40-fathom ledge around Kahanahaiki. Not long into our new course, we have yet another strike. But this one breaks the rubber band on the outrigger, and the reel screams as the line flies despite the drag. This is a *serious* fish, and captain and crew prepare for the fight. Leilani grabs the wheel as Kimo bounds down the ladder. Wow, some action! Bill tells me to start reeling in the other lines. Kaipo is out of his bunk and up on deck, rubbing his sleepy eyes, getting ready to *fight.* But something is wrong, and Kimo grimaces as he watches the line, realizing it was a plastic bag that triggered the outrigger. He heads back up the ladder to take the wheel, leaving it to Bill to remove the plastic and reset the rig. Bill laughs as he works, saying that was "for practice." I let the lines back out, Kaipo returns to his bunk, and Leilani returns to her reading.

10:15 a.m. Bill eloquently and accurately reminds me that fishing is "all about hours of boredom and moments of chaos and confusion." He wonders aloud about the odds of snagging a plastic bag as we did. But he opens a bag of chips and a soda as he speaks, then stops, and with an impish expression on his face, looks up at me and then back down at his plastic bag and plastic soda bottle. He laughs at his own behavior, tacitly acknowledging the ubiquity of plastic in modern society. I laugh with him; he is a funny man.

Bill remarks about the relatively recent changes in the process of finding and reporting one's position on the ocean. He says that dialogue between captains is changing from words (i.e., description of triangulating landmarks and underwater features) to numbers (i.e., exact degrees per the bearings on digital GPS readouts).

We initially heard various radio transmissions about others catching fish at about the same time as our own good fortune. But the airwaves and our own venture seem to have grown very quiet during the last hour. Bill remarks that when the bite is on, it often seems to last for just a little while, and then everything goes quiet again for some hours until numerous boats will again suddenly get "back into the thick of it." "It's like they slam the door shut, turn off the machine," he says.

The birds we followed have all but disappeared now, and the ocean and air above our path is quiet. But just as I note the quiet environs, a pod of jet-black, short-finned pilot whales (*Globicephala macrorynchus*) suddenly breach just off the port side, breaking the surface with a foamy swish and blowing their aerated seawater with a loud blast. Kimo points to the group and yells, "Puka heads!" in a manner that might be used if they presented an immediate danger to us. *Puka,* pronounced "poo-kah," means hole or perforation in Hawaiian, indicative of the large blowhole characteristic of this species. Leilani twists around quickly to get a view, and Kaipo briefly pops his head out of the cabin. Bill tells me the creatures are a bad sign and may be the reason why the bite has diminished in the last hour. He calls them the "vacuum cleaners of the ocean" because they tend to eat baitfish that would otherwise attract the pelagic species we now target.

Kimo is back on the radio now, this time talking with Bryan Sakai, a well-respected local Japanese charter captain who operates from Town (Honolulu). The conversation is short, but it is clear the two captains are well acquainted:

Kimo: Hey Bruddah Bryan, howseet going to-day?

Bryan: Ah, pretty good, pretty good, brah. . . . Jess peek ahp wahn ah-hee. . . . Good size . . . mehbee whan twahn-tee, whan ter-tie. . . . We happy now you know. [We just picked up a tuna, weighing maybe 120 or 130 pounds. We're happy now.]

Kimo: [Pause] Ah, dats good, dats good. . . . We just messing around da ledge dis morning. . . . Peek ahp some small ah-ku . . . suppah [supper].

Bryan: [Pause] Rah-jah, Rah-jah. . . . We go hunting sahm mo-ah. . . . Go peen-na-cool side. [Roger, Roger, we're going over toward the pinnacle to look around.]

Kimo: Rah-jah, rah-jah brah. . . . Go get 'em!.

Bryan: Okay . . . yeah . . . we go. . . . Catch up wit you lay-dah.

Kimo: 'Kay . . . out.

When the conversation is over, Bill leans over and says that Bryan is a really good fisherman—one of the most productive in the Islands—and that he doesn't know how Bryan does it. He then backpedals a bit to say that actually he *does* know, that "he works his butt off." A nice boat apparently helps, too, allowing him to quickly reach points around the south and west sides of the Island when the fish are biting there and then taking him back home to Town at the end of the day. I make a mental note, based on observation during this and other trips, about the lack of animosity between small-vessel captains, like Kimo, and charter captains who have bigger boats and an added source of income from their charters.

Indeed, the relationships are typically very good and mutually beneficial. As long as one captain trusts the judgment and experience of another, each may use the information provided by the other. In this regard, sometimes the manner of operation or ethnicity of captain just doesn't matter so much.

Being relatively new to these waters, I can't get over the immense depth here, even just a mile or so offshore. The water is an inky purple, filling an unimaginable abyss. I say as much to Bill, who replies accurately that "in Florida, you have to get up at three in the morning to get to water this deep!"

At about 11:40, a sleepy-eyed but invigorated Kaipo emerges from belowdecks, throwing a fish-embroidered pillow back onto the bunk as he emerges from the doorway. He stretches slowly and yawns, bringing life back into his tired limbs before slowly climbing the ladder to talk to his mother and father. He takes an orange from the cooler and peels as he talks and listens to his parents. Bill watches and feigns superstitious concern about the presence of oranges on board but says, "Now, if it was a banana, *then* I would worry!"

We reach the vicinity of the ledge around noon and begin to assume a northerly course again. With the sun now piercing more moderate depths along the ledge, the ocean assumes the color of brilliant cobalt, with even brighter azure visible closer to shore where large sandy deposits beckon swimmers out from the beaches. We continue for a short while and then turn to the south again. Shortly thereafter, a random radio report offers some encouragement, informing that a boat to the south of us has picked up an ono. *Au Punahele* hugs the ledge closely as Kimo uses a combination of fish-finder and visual reconnaissance to stay in what he deems is the right spot. Birds pass by, flying in various directions, but these wouldn't qualify as a pile; the stragglers are searching for baitfish as avidly as the captain of *Au Punahele* seeks big fish. But Kimo tires of the effort, offers the wheel to his son, and reclines a bit on the next seat over. We continue to troll, passing Malia, then Kaoa Cave, Ohiki, and La'a. As we round the bend just south of the Beach Park, I decide we are probably headed in to port for a short day. It is getting hot, and the earlier action is becoming a distant memory.

To Harbor

Passing a popular surf spot, I can see some longboarders catching tiny south swells breaking inside the reef. The swell is small, but the ocean looks refreshing. Kimo asks me about my surfing interests, and we talk surf story for a bit. Rugged Lanilai Point rises along our port side at about 1:00 p.m., the small swell crashing on its little islets as we pass. The harbor is now visible in the distance, though slightly obscured by heat waves rising from the still, glassy surface on this unusually calm day. If we're going to pick up an ono, we had better do it quickly! But it has become obvious our fishing will soon be pau (finished). Without cue, Kaipo starts reeling in the lines—the small aku centers first, then the corners on outriggers. Kimo climbs down to reel in the center and sides, leaving Leilani to navigate the remaining half-mile or so to the channel. Kimo then returns to the wheel, and Leilani assists in stowing the radio and depth finder while Kaipo and Bill swing in the outriggers to prepare for dockage. We pass the channel marker at 1:38, throttle down, and navigate into the harbor, settling into the slip at 1:42 p.m.

Rahb 'Em, Scrahb 'Em, Caht 'Em, Cleen 'Em

Once the engine is silenced, Kaipo cleats off the vessel, with some recommendations for fine adjustment from his father. Then he grabs the hose and begins a protracted period of cleanup. Leilani departs the vessel and makes her way up to the dockhouse to talk with the harbormaster's wife, also Native Hawaiian. Bill helps Kaipo clean the rods, reels, bat, and gaff. Everything is thoroughly rinsed, and the deck is scrubbed with a brush on a long handle, as is the fish box and entire surface of the vessel. I repeatedly offer to help but am refused; it seems guests are excused from these duties.

Kaipo and Bill continue their cleaning tasks while Kimo lifts the engine hatch and has a look, checking the oil and transmission fluid levels and probably making mental notes for what might be needed prior to the next voyage. Kaipo gets a little unwieldy with the hose around his father and is scolded once more. A strong and wise paternal influence is noted throughout this trip.

Kimo goes belowdecks to grab a cutting board, then reaches into the fish box for the aku and takes them to the dock to clean. He is adept, and after a series of well-practiced cuts on the board atop the dock box, he has produced a pile of nice, deep-red aku filets. The scraps go into the harbor to be fought over and picked at by various small fish and crabs waiting below. The captain separates the meat into three bags, the largest for his 'ohana, one for Bill, and one for me. I ask Kimo if he's sure there is enough to share with me. He replies forcefully and significantly in the affirmative, saying, "Dass da way we do eet."

I offer my cleaning services one last time, but I know they won't be accepted. I shake hands with Bill, who says, "Don't forget us on your way up, 'cause you might be coming back down!" I say good-bye and good luck to Kaipo, and finally to Kimo, shaking hands shakka style.[1] My summer trolling trip with this shy but kind Native Hawaiian 'ohana is pau (finished).

[1]This style of handshake is the norm among locals in Hawai'i. It is also common among many surfers in certain coastal towns around the United States, and so I have used it for many years. Its roots are undoubtedly Hawaiian; traveling surfers have brought the custom back to their beach homes on the Continent. The shakers' hands approach in a manner more open and angled more vertically than is the case with the tight-fingered and horizontally positioned "English" style. The positional aspect of the shakka-style shake requires that the involved thumbs interlock. This is the first phase. The second phase is enacted soon after—this is actually the English version—with hands horizontally positioned, thumbs adjacent. The third phase seems to be used only sometimes. That is, when the second phase is finished and the shakers' hands are sliding backwards from each other's grasp, the ends of the fingers of each are curled in a quick meeting—one last gesture. The occasion of this last gesture seems significant, but I have little evidence to support my understanding that it connotes a deeper phase of "interpersonal appreciation," if that is an accurate appraisal. In some cases, the last phase will be enacted quite forcefully, perhaps with a rapid departure of the hands, producing a kind of snap. I have no sense of the antiquity of this general style of phased handshake, though I suspect the third phase is a relatively recent development, used more frequently among youth. Between the time of the fieldwork and editing phases of this case study, a new change is evident among some youthful locals, wherein the final phase has been replaced with a mutually light forward knocking of the knuckles of the shakers' closed fists.

Keiki ready for go holoholo, O'ahu, 1999

Analysis

In my social anthropological reckoning, the outstanding feature of this trip is that although fishing is very important to Kimo, it is necessarily a sideline to what he is dedicated to on a daily basis—work on land (in this case, teaching). Bill is an exception, of course, because he's dedicated to fishing as a way of making a living. But for the 'ohana, the trip is a kind of escape from work—a common feature of "recreational" fishing in the United States. In a way, Bill's presence augments this as he's available to help if things get heavy (imagine how different this trip would have been had we hooked up with a 500-pound marlin—a very real possibility). But there is much more to it for these folks, since the tradition of fishing runs deep in their family and among their people, and they know it and love it.

Based on prolonged observation of fishing in this area, it is fairly unusual for a woman to go along, particularly among local fishermen. But it is not unheard of, and this trip had a strong family perspective with some history of direct participation by all members of the 'ohana, male and female alike. Leilani did not take an active role in fishing, but she was welcome and convivial, if somewhat quiet on board. Further, she was available to and did assist in navigating when needed, suggesting she may have had more to contribute had the trip assumed a different nature (i.e., more and bigger fish on the line).

This trip resulted in relaxing on the ocean and catching fish to eat. Kaipo found rest for his judo-weary limbs; Leilani read much of her book under the warm summer sun. Kimo successfully hunted for fish, talked to friends on the radio, and spent time with his family. Bill enjoyed himself, finding in me an outlet for conversation and humor, however practiced, and a chance to cruise offshore, beer in hand, fish occasionally on the line, and marine life in sight.

Fun and relaxation were undoubtedly motivating factors, and although the trip was successful in granting these, labeling the venture a purely "recreational" trip would detract from its food gathering and other attributes. Catching fish to eat was a compelling factor, and the fish that *were* caught would indeed be consumed by the ʻohana. Obviously, one can buy fish at market, and more cheaply than running the *Au Punahele* for half a day for a couple of aku. But two important factors should be considered here. First, catching, gathering, or harvesting food for consumption by the ʻohana can afford a dimension of subjectively experienced satisfaction not easily described in either qualitative or quantitative terms but a dimension that undoubtedly surpasses the supermarket experience. Fulfillment resulting from pursuing and bringing home fish from the boat is especially keen for Native Hawaiian fishermen, who report that taking fish or other seafood affords pili ana (connection) between human and natural worlds that is reportedly profound but not easily expressed. Members of this ʻohana love to eat and share fish. They will freeze big catches and immediately distribute smaller ones to family and neighborhood relations. When it's time for a wedding or lūʻau or funeral, Kimo reports he is ready with fish, for only fish will do for such occasions. Sharing keeps the family well integrated with their very ocean-oriented neighbors along this stretch of coast. Their willingness to share is both expected and reciprocated. But it is also respected as part of a local ethic of aloha (love and sharing), and it instills some measure of social status.

Second, there was the possibility throughout the course of the trip of catching a large fish or multiple large fish. Indeed, that was desired. Had this occurred, the relaxing attributes of the trip would necessarily have been abandoned in response to hana paʻa. Clearly, the eventualities of the trip, uncertain at the outset, determine its ultimate demeanor and scientific typing thereof. In this case, few fish coming up allowed for an extended period of relaxation, and the aku that did come up provided some satisfaction through catching fish for food. Thus, it is unclear, in the case of *Au Punahele,* at what point recreation is abandoned for work toward subsistence or whether recreation remains a part of subsistence. Of course, Kimo's status as a successful teacher may lead some to argue that this kind of fishing is not subsistence fishing *per se,* as undertaken on a daily basis in ancient times and by other Native Hawaiians around the Islands today. But Bill says that Kimo is generally disinclined to sell his catch and typically will smoke large marlin and freeze large ʻahi for personal and ʻohana consumption, rather than carry it to the market for sale. He loves to eat fish that he catches and to share it with others. This fact, combined with the spiritual or naturalistic aspect of catching fish to eat, as experienced by Native Hawaiians (and others, including other Native peoples and also non-Native peoples), argues for a more comprehensive definition of "subsistence."

The trip was an opportunity for subjective experience of another sort that also calls for some discussion. Being on the ocean and away from land, traffic, and noise is a special experience even in the absence of catching fish. Being on the ocean can enable a kind of spiritual experience, if such must or can be labeled. While drifting toward Ka Lae Loa above the vivid blue depths and mysterious creatures swimming below, with the ominous current outside and the greenest of mountains soaring above, it's easy to feel awe of the natural world and transcendence of mundane life. Can such an experience be incentive to come here to fish? In my own case it can and does, and although I cannot observe the internal workings of others, I must infer that others may at times experience the surroundings in a manner like mine.

From a more grounded and pragmatic analytical perspective, it is notable that this day's trip was relatively short. Apparently the captain saw no sense in continuing the trip under the hot sun when the night's dinner was in the fish box and more and/or bigger fish were not "jumping in the boat," as the saying goes. Kimo's attention to the radio conversations of other captains and his own conversations with them revealed that few fish were being landed in the near vicinity, apparently furthering his decision to call it quits. Kimo also offered information to another captain about his own aku catch, further evincing his participation in a social network of fishermen who cooperate toward success. Conversation with others is not limited to strategy, however. It often assumes the form of mere conversation, like Kimo's friendly words with Bryan. Camaraderie is notable; there is mutual understanding between fishermen who love the sea, the hunt for fish, and the challenges these present.

Kimo and family were quiet, but I didn't perceive my presence as cause for this. Kimo is quite eloquent but seems naturally reserved, and Kaipo is intelligent and well spoken but often quiet. Leilani was almost silent. These attributes lent to peaceful interaction on board. An exception to this was Kimo's scolding of Kaipo when he failed in some duty or another. But the situations surrounding the scolding were important and seemingly worth a word from any wise and caring father. The ocean this summer day was also quiet. The swell and wind were minimal; there was little boat traffic and, unfortunately, not much in the way of fish. The venture embodied recreation, but the motivations and empirical realities were at once more complex and simple than that term suggests, as expressed by Kimo himself:

> Dass whass nice 'bout my teaching. Can get out wit da fam-ah-lee, try get some feesh fo-ah eat, enjoy da waddah, all lie dat. [That's what's nice about my teaching career. I can get out with my family in the summer, catch some fish to eat, enjoy the water with them, and all that surrounds that.]

4/Hard-Core Commercial Trolling

It is not at all unusual for small-boat trollers in Hawai'i to sell some of their catch. The fish auction and other venues facilitate the sale of fish, and thus, many people fish commercially at least some of the time to supplement income from land-based job (or vice versa). Full-time troll operations are relatively rare. This undoubtedly relates to the fact that, in the long term, small-boat fishing is often not very rewarding in economic terms. So why participate on a full-time basis? Undoubtedly, the attractions of the lifestyle are what keep people involved: independence from a boss and the land-based workweek, meeting the challenges of the sea, basic enjoyment of a life on the ocean. This chapter describes both the difficulties of fishing commercially from small boats on a full-time basis and a range of factors that help explain the persistence of those who do not give up.

SOME HISTORY

Although fishing for money began long ago in distant regions, fish and fishing were central to economic transactions in ancient Hawai'i as well. During the earliest periods of society in the Islands, populations were generally small, and fishing was primarily consumption oriented. Because relatively few persons lived in any one ahupua'a in ancient times, there was probably relatively little strain on food resources, so deep-sea fishermen might go fishing as little as once a week. Goto (1986:471) suggests that in the early years of settlement, the production, consumption, and distribution of seafood were probably organized around kin relations.

But as new mariners arrived from other parts of Polynesia, ali'i (chiefly nobility) began to set up more complex societies, and surplus economies developed. Residents specialized in various economic and food production activities, such as fishing and upland taro production (Sahlins 1989). These activities were required for homage to the ali'i, and for purposes of subsistence and trade with others in the mauka (mountain) portions of a given ahupua'a and with people inhabiting other areas and islands. Among revered individuals were the konohikis (resource managers), some of whom cared for shoreline and ocean resources and activities, and the lawai'a haku (master fishermen). By the time Cook sailed into Kealakekua Bay on Hawai'i Island for the second and final time in 1779, a complex society had developed in the island region, with at least 276,000 indigenous residents (Nordyke 1989:18). Some experts assert that this number may have been much higher. Fishing was central to many aspects of social life.

As is well and tragically documented, following contact with the European explorers, Hawaiian society was increasingly disrupted through introduced disease, displacement of people and economic systems, the attractions and pitfalls of a cash economy and new materials, and a hegemonic and partly forced shift toward a Protestant work ethic, however syncretic with the indigenous system of beliefs and ways of living (I'i 1973). Certain beliefs and ways of living were not abandoned in full, however, but rather subverted, only to surface later and right up to the present. Of course, these sometimes surfaced in an altered state, but such is the evolving nature of culture and such was the nature of culture in Hawai'i (and elsewhere) long before the arrival of Cook.

With respect to interaction with the then-new cash economy, Native Hawaiians were actually leaders in innovative commercial fishing methods and production, from the whaling period (1820–1865) into the beginning of the Territorial Days. Schug (2001:5) notes the continuity of fishing during this period:

> As new goods and materials became available, Hawaiian fishermen modified their accoutrements . . . [but] retained many of the long-established techniques that were so well-adapted to Hawai'i's marine environment. Also retained were various ancient rituals to ensure safety at sea and a bountiful catch. . . . Commercial fishing provided Hawaiians an early opportunity to participate in the new island economy with relatively small capital outlay and without abandoning their own customs and skills.

Scobie (1949:288) reports on U.S. Commission of Fish and Fisheries statistics and notes that of the 2,345 persons who sold fish in Hawai'i in 1901, 1,571 were Native Hawaiians, 485 were of Japanese ancestry, and 238 were of Chinese ancestry. Participation of Native Hawaiians in commercial fishing gradually diminished, however, and Japanese immigrants increasingly took to the sea to fish in the first years of the new century. Eventually, gasoline and diesel-powered engines were adapted for use on the sampans, and fishermen of Japanese ancestry effectively intensified the commercial possibilities of deep sea fishing in Hawai'i.

Differences in approaches to fishing between the Hawaiians and newly arriving fishermen were both cultural and social structural. First, the Hawaiians only partially engaged the ideologies and competitive demands associated with the new cash economy. Their manner of fishing undoubtedly tended to satisfy a mix of motivations involving the consumption and sharing of fish in the extended family setting and the sale of seafood to generate cash to be used for various family and community needs. Second, the Hawaiians were fragmented in a social structural sense. People were displaced both geographically and ideologically, and they often struggled against the purveyors of the haole (foreign) ways. There were strong interests in tradition, attractions to new ways and items, and syncretism of these. To be sure, there was an ongoing focus on subsistence practices, using both traditional and newfound methods.

Meanwhile, as Schug notes (2002:8–12), the *issei* or first-generation immigrants employed gear strategies traditionally used in Japan. These included long-line methods, first used offshore O'ahu around 1917. The issei eventually expanded their range and operations, largely through fiscal and social capital made available within and among extended families and a cultural system that appears to have been attuned to capitalism. Japanese immigrants also became successful in seafood marketing businesses, and many fishermen of the same ancestry were assisted in their fishing operations via credit arrangements with the wholesalers.

Small-boat commercial fishing success enjoyed by the issei and the *nissei,* or second generation, was quickly stifled during World War II. Many sampans were confiscated, and nearshore and offshore waters were restricted and heavily patrolled by U.S. forces.

The small-boat fleet blossomed again after the war and into the present day. Today, many Native Hawaiian, local Japanese, local Pacific Islander, local Filipino, local Portugese, local Puerto Rican, local Korean, and other kama'āina and newly arriving small-boat captains and crew fish from small boats around the Islands. Despite the general popularity of small-boat fishing in Hawai'i today, however, fishing for a living here is as challenging as it ever was and probably more so, as described in the following case.

PREVIEW

The high mountains that rise abruptly along the leeward coastlines of the Hawaiian Islands minimize the effect of predominant east and northeast trade winds. During normal trade conditions, this makes for ideal boating in close proximity to the shore, with increasingly rougher conditions typical farther from land. Good sea surface conditions, public launching facilities, and reputations for good fishing make the leeward waters particularly popular spots to fish. This is cetainly the case in summer, when the 'ahi bite is on and many people have free time to get out on the water. Captains trailer their vessels from all over the island to fish in the area.

But even on any given day in winter, fishermen of varying experience and knowledge can be found searching for fish in the offshore waters of Hawai'i. There are experts and novices, boats that give wide berth and boats that pass too closely, hopeful captains and determined captains, FAD fishermen and chasers of birds, cruisers and workers, cooperative fishermen and some loners. There are also the few hard-core fishermen who go to sea with profit motive in mind and who will work long hours until fish are found, caught, and marketed.

THE HARD-CORE TROLL TRIP

Most of the fishermen who participated in this study work on a full- or part-time basis at various land-based jobs. But many retain flexibible positions, and fish when they have or make time. Relatively speaking, there are only a handful of full-time or what might be called "hard-core" smallboat fishermen here whose lives revolve around preparing to fish and fishing on a primarily commercial basis. License data files indicate that some 285 full-time small-vessel commercial captains were active in the Islands during the late 1990s.

The relative scarcity of full-timers and the fact that they are almost always at sea or preparing to depart makes them very hard to contact. Once, when I felt I was getting close to a prospective informant, his engine developed problems and my contact told me the boat would be out of action for some time—to give it a rest. Finally, after nearly three months of my patient waiting, my contact said it might be a good time to try. I finally reached the prospective informant by telephone, and we made some tentative plans for me to participate in an upcoming trip. But alas, the weather went bad the next day, and the high winds of winter precluded small-vessel fishing for a couple more weeks! When the winds abated, I spoke once again with the elusive captain and things looked hopeful, though he questioned my experience and whether I was prone to seasickness because, as he said, "Once we wen get going, we go, eh?" ["Once we shove off, there is no turning back. Do you understand?"] I reassured him, and he suggested I come to the dock the following Sunday to meet and to "look at da boat." But this meeting failed, too; after a long drive to the harbor from Town, I found the vessel and docks empty at the prescribed meeting time! We talked again the next Tuesday. He was somewhat apologetic and offered, "We go soon, brah." So it seemed that the missed meeting actually worked to my advantage. But the weather failed again, and another week passed until solid plans were made under clear skies and calm winds to make the trip the following day, late in February 1999.

Real Time: Preparations Long Underway

I arrive at the pier ten minutes shy of the 5:30 a.m. rendezvous time, having left home at 4:30. The wind is calm and the sunrise still an hour away. The engine on the *Maile Kai* is already running. A spotlight above the to-bridge ladder illuminates the deck but makes it hard to see anything above eye level. But I can see the hands of captain and crew, and I shake them. Greetings are cordial but brief, with serious countenance. Captain Pilipo (pronounced "Pee-lee-poh") immediately puts me to task helping first mate Lahi (pronounced "Lah-hee") load ten 20-pound bags of ice into the fish box while David unloads rods and reels from belowdecks and inserts them into their respective rod holders along the stern. The captain hands me an unsheathed knife to cut the tops off the plastic ice bags for rapid loading into the box. He then moves to other unseen tasks on the bridge. Lahi stands on the finger pier above and hands down the bags in succession from an iron loading cart. Dumping the tenth bag, I use my numbing fingers to spread out the ice in the box. Feeling uncertain and in the way, I then step into the shadows in the starboard stern corner and watch. Pilipo gingerly carries the GPS and radio from storage below, up the ladder to the bridge, and installs them as David finishes with the rods.

Preparations continue, captain and crew going about a well-rehearsed routine. Finally, the captain looks about the boat. Everyone is now standing still,

Early morning departure for the trolling grounds, O'ahu

and it appears all is ready. Pilipo looks my way and asks, "Eh, brah, what exactly you doing again?" Everyone turns toward me to listen. I explain my research interest in the everyday life of fishermen and how going fishing is the best way to go about learning, that I'd been on various trips around the Islands and had learned a lot, and so forth. This seems to satisfy the captain, and I suspect the explanation jibes with that of my contact, who had previously filled Pilipo in on the purpose and nature of the study. The captain immediately launches into discussion about the unseen effort involved in preparation for the current trip. He says the trip had actually begun the previous afternoon when he changed the engine oil and then worked until almost 1:30 a.m. making various other preparations for today, rising at 3:30 a.m. to pack lunch and begin his trip to the harbor.

Just then a haole (Caucasian) fisherman named Mike emerges from the shadows into the spotlight and greets Pilipo with distinctly local speech. He is somewhat wet and dirty and looks tired. Pilipo and Mike shake hands "shakka" style and talk briefly about Mike's fishing trip the previous day and evening. Pilipo introduces me and my agenda, and Mike quickly asks, "Is it gonna hurt us or help us?" making evident the solidarity between these fishermen and the sensitive nature of the small-vessel enterprise in a context of competition between user groups. With my back to the spotlight and facing the four fishermen awaiting an answer (two with knives in hand), what else would I say? My "help," might have sounded like a "gulp," but I meant it, as I believe that describing the realities of this kind of fishing lifestyle will contribute to more educated decisions about its management. Duties out of the way and conversation with Mike waning, Pilipo abruptly but audibly states, "We go."

As Mike disappears into the darkness of the harbor, I let loose the starboard stern lines while Lahi works the bow. The vessel drifts slowly backward with guidance from Pilipo at the controls up on the bridge. I am surprised to see

David left behind on the pier. He came early to help in the preparations, but was not fishing today—laulima. With a quick thrust of forward power and a spin of the wheel to starboard, Lahi, Pilipo, and I motor to the harbor entrance. Lahi releases the side outriggers from their inactive positions. It is 5:55 a.m.

Sea-Bound with Pilipo and Lahi

Pilipo is a rather short man with a powerful build, seemingly possessing a mix of ethnic/genetic heritage, Hawaiian and Japanese certainly. But such matters are insignificant at this hour—constructs of an overly analytical social scientist perhaps. For Pilipo is patently *local* in speech, in dress, in manner. Having grown up on O‘ahu and fishing offshore most of his 56 years, Pilipo's extensive knowledge of the island's offshore waters is second nature to him. That such knowledge is relatively new to me may actually be an advantage for the sake of research, for I find myself inquisitive and observant of all that he takes for granted in fishing, in interaction with others, in life.

Lahi is also part-Native Hawaiian and local in speech, dress, and manner. He wears a sleeveless T-shirt, and a tattoo of the Hawaiian Islands spreads across his upper back. At about 6 feet and powerful in build, the young man is quite handy when a task of strength is required. Pilipo comments on his good vision—imperative in the search for feeding birds while trolling. In contrast to Pilipo, who talks constantly on the radio, Lahi is very quiet, speaking few words on few occasions, tending rather to nod and point rather than talk. His eyes are constantly on the horizon.

The sun is still well below that horizon as we head offshore, the cool air and soft salty spray waking me a bit. A nearly full moon sets in the west, illuminating the sea around us and the deck of the boat below our feet. The ocean is extraordinarily calm, with only a 4-foot north swell detectable at about a 12-second interval and virtually no surface chop. Pilipo and Lahi sit behind the windshield at the bridge, and Pilipo asks me to join them on a bench seat directly behind.

Something seems amiss in Pilipo's countenance and behavior as I approach the seat. He stares at me and then at my feet. I can't guess what it is. He holds out his hand as if to shake shakka style, and I do so. We enter into the shake, but as I begin to withdraw my hand, he maintains the grip, looks in my eyes, and says, "Good luck, bruddah, I wish you good luck." I smile and thank him, but I'm puzzled! This is his boat and trip. I am a mere observer and he knows that; I should be wishing *him* luck. But then he looks down at my feet again and then back into my eyes and says with a smile, "Hey, brah, old Japanese kah-stahm—we no way-ah slee-pahs on da boat . . . eez bad lah-ck. . . . Da boat is home, you know." Still smiling, he releases his grip, and we finish the handshake. Somewhat embarrassed, I quickly remove and stow my rubber slippers (depending on one's region, also known as sandals, slaps, or flip-flops; they are also called zoris in Hawai‘i).

Returning to sit, I ponder the mistake. I knew that foot coverings are kapu (forbidden) in most if not all houses in Hawai‘i, but it never occurred to me that this would be the case on board, and no other captain had mentioned it during previous trips. But at that point I hadn't fished with a captain of part-Japanese ancestry. The event added a layer of complexity to my simplistic notion of "local," in that other local captains had not felt wearing slippers a problem, yet this local captain made sure all aboard went barefoot. I've since learned much more about cultural subtlety within and across ethnic groups in the Islands and wish to warn that the haole (foreigner) invariably lacks basic knowledge about a complex society of which locals are always highly knowledgeable. Humility is indispensable, and haole-centrism is anathema.

The captain is friendly and talkative despite my faux pas, and it seems that his handshake and wish for luck somehow erased or purged the brief period during which I had violated the custom. But then Pilipo remembers to ask me with equal parts sincerity and humor, whether I had brought any bananas aboard! "No, no bananas today," I reply forcefully and with laughter, knowing of *that* superstition (and old tune). "Dat's good brah, dat's good," he laughs, "We vehhhhry soo-pah-stee-shuss on dis boat. . . ." Lahi peers at the dark horizon, unsmiling.

Pilipo talks about his operation as we motor slowly westward at about 3 knots. I scribble notes in the moonlight. The captain says that the currents were extraordinarily strong between the Islands during the last few days, and he's been burning a lot of fuel. In preparation for this particular trip, he reports having spent $60 for fuel; $30 for food, drinks, and smokes; and $20 for ice (it must be mentioned in retrospect that fuel prices would almost triple over the few years following my conversation with the captain). This led to a discussion that was to continue periodically throughout the trip of the economic challenges of running a small trolling operation.

Sunrise: Light on Boat and Water

By 6:15 a.m., the sun begins to illuminate the east side of the mountain range while obscuring the moon, now barely visible in the direction of Japan. It seems we have reached the appropriate position for putting lines in the water. Although the vessel is guided by interaction of GPS and autopilot, I am asked to watch out for logs while the captain and mate negotiate the ladder down to the stern to let out the lines. Collision with a log or other large object could be deadly. Our course is 210 degrees (southwest) and forward speed has been increased to 7.4 knots. There is no electronic fish-locating device aboard.

At about 13 feet in beam and 32 feet in length, Pilipo's boat is relatively stable and comfortable. The forward semi-vee 1969 model fiberglass hull does well in seas and is sufficiently powered by an 8-cylinder 8.2-liter diesel. The vessel was purchased in 1994 for $48,000. The belowdecks, including the forward vee berth, appear organized but largely unused. Drawers and cabinets hold various gear and standard safety devices. A wheel, throttle, and other controls enable navigation from below with vision through a forward-facing belowdecks window, an invaluable option in rough weather. Otherwise, navigation occurs from the bimini-covered tower, roughly 12 feet above waterline.

The stern deck space is open, with no fighting chair. But the centrally positioned engine hatch is elevated to about 14 inches, and a rubber mat enables its use as a platform for landing and dispatching fish. The fish box sits on the starboard side, while a large cooler is situated to port. The entire stern deck is about 10 feet square and covered with an aluminum-framed bimini, about 7 feet above the deck. Various bats and gaffs are located in close proximity to the fish-landing area, and a hose allows for cleaning of the space after landing fish.

With respect to gear, Pilipo is equipped to catch big fish. Lahi drops the center line and lure first, attached to one of five massive and somewhat weathered 16/0 reels. This is let out to around 85 yards or so, as marked with red ink on the 130-pound test line, and then attached to the center outrigger situated behind my seat on the bridge. Interestingly, the center outrigger is attached to "spider lines" that are, in turn, attached to the side outriggers. By keeping an eye on the motion of the spider lines, Pilipo says he can often tell if something is pursuing the lures on any of the outriggers. Pilipo lets out the port side reel to about 75 yards and attaches it to the port outrigger. The process is repeated on the other side of the boat. The starboard corner is let out next, not quite as far as the sides—perhaps to about 65 yards. The port corner line is let out to roughly the same distance. Finally, the stern lines are let out to about 50 yards. These are attached to two much smaller reels mounted on small stainless-steel mounts rather than rods. The lures used on these rigs are notably smaller than the others as they are intended for smaller fish, such as aku and small 'ahi, also known as shibi.

Hunt for the Bird Pile and Conversation at Sea

We are fishing by 6:20 a.m., still headed southwest. With the captain back at the bridge, Lahi at his side, and the ocean increasingly visible, we commence a search for feeding birds that is to last the entire day. Both Pilipo and Lahi make use of small but high-powered binoculars with good optics. Mine are powerful, but the relatively poor optics make it difficult to keep a steady gaze on the horizon.

The captain lights a cigarette, his eyes peering into the distance. He occasionally alters our course a degree or two so as to cut through the swells at the most comfortable angle. I ask him how long he's been fishing. This elicits a long conversation about many aspects of his operation. He says that he's been fishing all of his life but was "put out to pasture" from his union job as a heavy equipment operator five years prior and decided to put his savings into fishing, so he would have some way to make a living. He reports that his previous years of fishing were more leisurely in nature; he trailered to launch ramps and often fished solo, mostly on weekends. Now, if the weather is good, he will fish four or five times per week. Lahi usually goes along, but Pilipo will go solo, as necessary. But when I ask if there are conditions the captain won't brave, he says

> No mess wit Mah-dah Nay-tcha. . . . Had tree bad wahns arready you know . . . da one in da sixties almost sank 'em. . . . Try go out to terdy knots maybe, but aftah dat I'm pau arready brah.
>
> [I won't mess with Mother Nature. . . . I've had three near disasters already. I almost sank my boat during a bad blow in the 1960s. I will venture out to fish until the winds reach about 30 knots, but after that I consider it too rough and I won't go out.]

We're interrupted by a radio conversation between two other captains to which Pilipo listens intently, adjusting the squelch knob for better reception. The fishermen speak only briefly. The captain knows the speakers. They are retirees he calls "recree-ay-shun kine" [recreational types]. Desiring to understand his definition of that phrase, I ask if the fishermen to which he refers ever sell their fish. The captain replies that they do, but he bases his definition of "recreational" rather on their tendency to stay within 8 miles of the coast, with a primary focus on the 40-fathom ledge.

Suspecting that the fishermen in question may also tend toward subsistence/consumptive fishing and sharing of their catch, I ask Pilipo whether he, as a fisherman oriented toward profit, regularly eats or shares his catch. He reports that if the catch is meager, he will sell it anyway, asserting that "evree-ting helps." At first, this contradicts my sense that taking just a few "pieces" to market isn't worth the effort and expenditure of traveling and that eating it is the more rational option. But then I realize that Pilipo is trying to stress how tough it is to make it in the fishing business and that, in truth, he does on occasion eat and share a small portion of his catch, depending on the extent of that catch any given day. He says, "Sometime share da kine . . . but aftah while . . . geeving expensive you know. . . . Try go make money." ["I will share a part of my catch sometimes, but after awhile giving fish away is just too expensive. So I have to go primarily to make money."]

Of his ongoing investment in his gear and vessel, Pilipo notes significantly that everything that makes contact with the ocean—"evree-ting marine"—wears out quickly and must constantly be replaced. The captain reports having just spent $500 to fix his bridge bimini, ripped by birds in the harbor, and says he spends $3,000 to $6,000 every time his boat is taken out of the water for dry-dock repair.

Talk of money leads to talk of selling fish. The captain says he generally dislikes the auction process, asserting that it renders the small-boat captain powerless. If a troller desires to sell fish, he will take it to the auction to be sold that day or the next. If he feels it is of high quality, he can put a minimum price on the fish; it may be bought at a higher price but not lower. Thus, the fisherman risks the fish not being sold at all, in which case he may "eat" it (literally or figuratively), share it with others, or sell it elsewhere. According to Pilipo, buyers don't like the minimum price option, and they often tend to refuse it:

> Seven times een ten dey nevah buy 'em . . . no like meeneemum. . . . Dey black-ball you so fast brah . . . call you, say "Come peek em ahp." We at da mercy of da buyers. . . . Eez not da auction, eet's da buyers, brah, eez wahn mo-nah-poh-lee, eh?
>
> [Seventy percent of the time the buyers won't buy it. They don't like the minimum price option. They will cut you out of the market so fast, my friend. . . . They will call you to say "Come pick up your fish, we don't want it." We are at the mercy of the fish buyers. It's not the auction that is at fault, it's the buyers. The buyers constitute a monopoly that controls the market.]

No birds are visible at 6:55 a.m., but the radio is active. One of the calls is directed to Pilipo, but the signal is weak and the conversation short. All we can hear is, "Hey, kee-lah, he-ah you geev 'em yes-tah-day!" ["Hey, coolest, we heard you caught the big tuna yesterday."] Pilipo seems to have no time or interest in a detailed reply and merely asks, "Hey—who toll you dat?" Evidently, the caller is fishing in more ways than one, complimenting Pilipo (the mark) on a good day he might have had but actually seeking information about where he might have caught the fish. This leads the captain to make disparaging remarks about some local fishermen and their reliance on others, rather than on their own ability to find fish:

> Plenny guys' down-fall is dis black box, brah [pointing to the radio]. Dey follow dat instead of da feesh! Dey get off da game plan, yeah?
>
> [The downfall of many fishermen is reliance on reports coming over the CB radio. They follow what other people say about the fish rather than the fish themselves. They deviate from (what Pilipo sees as) the real mission of actually finding fish rather than talking about it all the time.]

I find this perspective interesting in that it seems to contradict Pilipo's own tendency to listen to and talk on the radio. He seems to value the conversations and reports of some captains above others, but it remains to be seen whether even valued reports affect his decisions about navigation and strategy of pursuit.

His next conversation, at 7:25 a.m., is with a charter-boat captain he seems to respect. They share information about recent trips and the strategies of the day. Unfortunately, the wind makes it difficult to hear the details. But when Pilipo finishes, he leans back to tell about a friend of his who is fishing with a back injury. Pilipo says with empathy, "You got to go feesh even when you hurt, brah. Got to try go make money, eh?" Evidently, the charter captain pulled muscles while gaffing a fish, and he told Pilipo that it hurts him now, especially when seas are choppy. This must remind Pilipo of his own ills, and he pulls a vial from his pocket and takes a pill for a chronic heart condition, washing it down with a soda. There is a chill in the air, and I cross my arms to gain some heat. We continue our hunt for birds.

Pilipo talks a little more about his fishing operation. He says that he will occasionally travel as far as a neighbor island but generally stays along this stretch of coast, engaging in trolling only. He says, "Like do what love best, eh?" ["I do what I love best, do you understand?"] Pilipo does not hide his economic motivations: "Nevah waste time wit any-ting . . . Eez hahd enuf, to make eet brah." ["It's really hard to make it in this business—I don't have time or money to waste with efforts that aren't productive."]

This makes me wonder what Pilipo might do if he couldn't fish, and what would happen to his family. He tells me he lives with his wife but that his two girls are married and living in other parts of O'ahu. Of his chosen occupation and other options he says:

> I 56 yeahs now, eh? What odda kine jobs I try get at dis age? No m-oah nah-ting. But not ready foah lay down en die, arready. I gone do *sahm-teeng*. Could try get well-faia . . . but no want dat. . . .
>
> [I am 56 years old now. What other types of employment could I feasibly look for at my age? There are no other options for me. I'm not ready to lie down and die! I have to do *something*. I could go on welfare, but that's not what I want.]

It is clear Pilipo has long contemplated his situation, and he has made some serious commitments to the fishing lifestyle.

With an ongoing research interest in the role of women in fishing, I decide to ask about his daughters and whether they have ever been involved in the operation. His answer plays into one of my suppositions about what is clearly a male-centered activity in the Islands (and elsewhere). I imagine with some amusement how the women might react to his assessment that they are better suited for other things.

For no apparent reason, we take a more westerly course just past 9:00 a.m. There are no birds about. Under the glare of the rising sun, both Pilipo and Lahi have put on polarized sunglasses and continue staring intently at the horizon. *My* eyes are already tired of the hunt.

I notice Pilipo glancing behind us once, then again a couple minutes later. I finally see what he sees, a boat on the distant horizon. By a few minutes after 10:00, it has gained considerably and is about a mile off our stern, a few degrees starboard.

Interaction: Defining "Leeway"

Pilipo likes seclusion while fishing. One motive is economic and obvious: If a school of fish is encountered, it is best encountered without competition. But I sense, too, that freedom and solitude are part of what he enjoys about fishing. Thus, Pilipo becomes increasingly irritated at the captain who is closing in on us. This is evinced by the tone of his voice while talking about our new adherent, his constant watch off the stern, and, ultimately, his evasive tactics—a series of protracted turns south and west. But the following vessel won't budge. Its captain copies our course for over an hour.

Meanwhile, Lahi has spotted some birds about 400 yards off our bow. By about 10:20 a.m., we are in the midst of a flock of small seabirds that divebomb the surface, feeding on tiny baitfish. There is a smell of fish in the air. The birds, the smell, and the textured water surface below them give a sense of place that in my reckoning has been absent all morning. The presence of life and movement on what to this point has been a glassy, relatively featureless ocean orients me somehow. Suddenly, we are *somewhere*!

Just then, the two center reels click and scream as aku take the two center lures. The lines rush out quickly with a "z-z-z-z-z-z-z-z-z-z!" Lahi bounds down the ladder in a flash as Pilipo throttles down just slightly and calls out, "How many?" "Two," replies Lahi. The mate quickly engages the reel gear and begins gathering in the line by hand in long, deliberate pulls without losing tension. I follow suit. Lahi reminds me to keep the line I have gathered between my feet and not under or behind them so as to avoid trouble with tangled appendages if the fish should overpower me. But just then my line goes slack, and we have only one fish on. I let the line back out as Lahi lands his fish with a small gaff and dispatches it with the gaff's butt end on the elevated engine cover. The 4-pound aku is immediately put in the cooler and covered with ice. Lahi then lets his line out and the captain throttles forward, back into the midst of the constantly moving bird pile.

Crowding Captain Pilipo at the bird pile, offshore O'ahu

Evidently our relatively erratic movements over the last minutes have been spotted by our follower, who recognizes them as signs of fish being landed. The boat is now less than a quarter-mile off our stern. This is far too close for Pilipo, who uses various muffled expletives to express his displeasure. But we keep fishing, and within ten minutes we have two more aku on the same lines. The landing process is repeated, although this time the fish on the line that is my kuleana (responsibility) is landed as well. By 11:00 a.m. we have five aku aboard, and the boat continues in the midst of the bird pile and just ahead of our dogged pursuer. The slow morning has woken up, and Lahi is visibly pleased and more talkative.

But suddenly, Pilipo, having had enough of our human remora,[1] guns the engine and directs the *Maile Kai* at the birds and feeding fish! The intensity of acceleration is such that Lahi and I are forced to hold on more forcefully than usual. Pilipo chases the birds and the school of fish until they disperse. Clearly, our fishing in this spot is pau [finished]! The spree is over as quickly as it began, leaving no reason for our follower to follow any longer. Such was the intention of our frustrated captain!

Lahi remains characteristically nonplussed and sets out to more carefully cover the fish with ice and icy brine—a frigid slurry that is optimal for preserving the fish. There is a tangible and positive change in Pilipo's demeanor as he adopts a new bearing of 169 degrees (south of west), away from humanity and toward a vacant horizon.

[1]Remora species (such as *Remora remora*) have developed the ability to attach themselves to larger creatures such as sharks or rays, and to benefit in various ways by the relationship.

A Change of Course and a Change of Seas

By about 1:00 p.m. we are thirty miles out of the harbor. The mountain range has diminished on the northeastern horizon, and there are no other vessels in sight. In another couple of hours or so, we will be well beyond sight of land. But Pilipo suddenly makes a 180-degree turn and the vessel heads back into the northerly swell at a bearing of 329 degrees. The captain is headed back in. The seas are a bit disorganized now, or so it seems traveling upwind. But the breeze *has* accelerated a bit under the heat of the midday sun. The boat does well, however, its bow easily carving seas and swell, with only splash and spray to indicate passage, its captain and crew unaffected.

Lahi and Pilipo continue their relentless search for birds while I sit behind them facing the stern and Samoa. There is a long period of silence. It is as if the change in our direction and the condition of the sea have again changed Pilipo's mood. His conversation has ebbed, and even the radio is turned off. He smokes a cigarette, puts it out, and then begins to nod off, his body shifting at an odd angle, his head to one side. When the boat hits a particularly large bit of chop, he rights himself, only to nod off again. Some forty minutes pass, during which not a word is spoken between us. Lahi takes the binoculars from his eyes only briefly.

The engine of a jet drones some 15,000 feet overhead, making its way between the Islands. I reflect on the difference between this world of solitude and the noisy commerce of Town. Just then, Pilipo awakens, seemingly refreshed by his nap, and mentions something about this being a good day for hebi (spearfish or *Tetrapterus angustirostris*). I wonder if he was dreaming about fish! He clarifies by telling me that the last time he was in this general vicinity, he landed a 47-pound hebi, and the water had the same reddish organic material floating about as we see now. Pilipo turns on the radio, and a barrage of disconnected conversations are discernible between the static. The captain listens and then begins a muffled conversation with a friend. I can hear only bits and pieces from either side:

Pilipo's friend: Ten-pound size mo bettah . . . [static]. . . . We untangling lines. . . . Try pick ahp bait . . . drag bait.

Pilipo: Good going brah, dat's wahn good day . . . [static]. . . . Rah-jah . . . Got good size aku . . . shibi. . . . Went up peen-nah-cool . . . no moah nah-ting.

Pilipo's friend: Evree day wahn new day. . . . Maybe get mo-ah lucky lay-dah. . . . Usually aftah-noon fish come ovah he-ah.

Pilipo: Da fish see evree-ting you know. . . . We nineteen miles out now. . . . Ahhh . . . going ahp sea now.

Pilipo's friend: Okay, ahhh . . . go get 'em. . . . We talk to you latah.

Pilipo: Ahhh, ohh-kayyy, rahhh-jah, rah-jah. . . . Out.

[PF: The ten-pounders are better to catch (and sell). . . . We are untangling our lines right now. . . . We're trying to catch some bait. . . . We're going to fish by using live-bait methods.

Lahi's relentless search for birds

P: Roger. . . . We caught some good-sized skipjack tuna. . . . (We're looking for) bigeye tuna. . . . We went to the pinnacle area. . . . We didn't catch anything.

PF: Every day is a new day. . . . Maybe you will have better luck later on. . . . The fish usually come over here in the afternoon.

P: The fish can see everything (today). . . . We're nineteen miles out right now. . . . Ahhh . . . we're going to head into the trade winds now.

PF: Okay, ahhh . . . good luck, go catch some fish. . . . We'll talk to you later on.

P: Ahhh, okay. Roger. Roger, out.]

The trade winds are picking up considerably now, and the vessel's collisions with each of the larger swells we encounter send salty spray to the bridge. We pass some rubbish as an isolated bird or two fly by. The presence of trash in the water leads Pilipo to talk about other objects attractive to fish, especially old nets and dead whales. I know from olfactory experience the latter are malodorous, but they are always accompanied by a host of creatures, including birds and fish. Pilipo talks excitedly of dead whales: "Whales, ohhh brah . . . whales . . . eh-vree whance een a while!"

By 3:00 p.m., the breeze has freshened and whitecaps abound. Clouds obscure the sun, and the ocean takes on a darker, more ominous hue. The (big) fish continue to elude us.

Heading In: Meeting the Behavioral Nexus of Commerce and Recreation

Despite the fact that the fishing is very slow, Lahi remains attentive to the horizon, perhaps more so as the day wears on. I sense strong economic imperative for success. But by 3:20 p.m., Pilipo shifts our northerly course significantly toward the east, assuming a bearing of about 35 degrees, apparently heading back toward the harbor. This makes sense if captain and crew hope to be home for dinner, because we are still about ten miles out. Meanwhile, there is a lot of activity on the radio, and Pilipo listens intently. Given the nature of the conversations, I reckon many vessels are winding up their day on the water and discussing their successes or lack thereof as they head back to land. One captain hails *Maile Kai* and, though I can barely make out what is said, I do hear Pilipo agree to take the man's aku to market later in the evening.

By a little after 4:00 p.m., the harbor is getting closer, now about six nautical miles to starboard. I point to a bird pile about a mile off the port side, leading the captain in pursuit. This seems a final effort to find fish while heading in. We reach the birds and make a large, slow circle and then another, but with no result. By the time we finish circumnavigating, the birds have dispersed and moved on. Although I can't read the faces of captain or mate, *I* feel frustrated and a bit tired of the hunt, and a small, weak voice in my head says, "Might as well head in now; we'll be in a little after five and cleaned up by six . . . I can make it home by seven. . . . We tried."

But somehow, strangely, while my mind was making for the harbor, the boat was heading back out to sea! I realized quickly, and made the proper mental adjustments, that our trip was not nearly over, that this was a trip for profit and not for "play." Thus, whereas most of my previous fishing experiences in Hawai'i had involved fewer hours at sea, this was something more—we had a mission, and it was important. I didn't mind so much. The sun was getting lower in the partly cloudy sky, and I knew it would make for a beautiful late afternoon, here between islands in the middle of the vast central Pacific.

Northbound: FADs and Payoff

Our new bearing is about 338 degrees, or somewhat west of north. Pilipo is headed for one of the FADs, now just a couple of miles away. We approach the round, yellow "can" from the east. Circling is fruitless once again, so we continue more directly northward toward the next buoy and Ka Lae Loa, searching unsuccessfully all the while for birds or any sign of fish.

Maile Kai reaches the northerly buoy around 5:15 p.m., amidst growing swells and choppy conditions. Moving walls of textured, deep-blue water obscure the buoy, then expose it. As we approach, I see that a cormorant (*Phalacrocoracidae spp.*) sits on top, unflinching. Again, Pilipo navigates a large, slow circle. But there is no action, and the captain and mate are silent as we eventually give up on this strategy as well and head farther north and slightly east toward the rocky lava headland at Ka Lae Loa.

It's not hard to see that Pilipo and Lahi are increasingly frustrated. Determined to appreciate the rest of the trip, I carefully climb down to the deck to get a different perspective on the seas and to get a drink. The view from belowdecks is obscured by vigorous pelting sprays of sea and wind. The swell grows as we approach the headland. The National Weather Service had predicted the arrival of a new northwest 10-foot swell from a moderately strong winter storm some 2,000 nautical miles to the northwest, and we seem to be experiencing its arrival.

At about 5:45 p.m., I notice a single bird flying about, the first we have encountered in some time. Just then, POW! "Z-z-z-z-z-z-z-z-z-z-z-z-z-z-z-z-z-z-z-z-z-z-z." HANA PA'A! We have a big fish on the corner line! Lahi is down the ladder in a flash, with a big smile on his face as he readies for the fight. The captain throttles down very slightly, and as I look up, I see a slight smile on his weathered visage as well. But the fight has just begun, and behavior aboard the *Maile Kai* has quickly transformed from silent watching to frenetic action. The captain remains ever composed, however, and calmly reminds me to reel in the other lines, customary when a big fish is on, reducing the possibility of tangling.

Lahi reckons the fish is a marlin but quickly changes his mind to mahimahi. I'm unsure how he can tell, but his second assertion is correct, and after the mate works the reel for about eight minutes, the captain comes down to assist in gaffing the creature—a bright yellow and apple-green fish that is really a fighter. Gaffing and landing are rendered difficult by the swell, which we now approach at a broad reach of about 30 degrees so as to reduce roll. The autopilot keeps us on course, and kōkua of captain and mate enables success as I stand prepared and take in the action. The fish is about 50 inches long and slaps vigorously on the moving deck. Pilipo quickly and deftly grabs an old blanket from a storage box and covers the fish to limit its movement, whereupon Lahi knocks it unconscious with repeated strikes with a small but hefty aluminum bat. He then runs a stiff wire through the brain cavity and into the spine of the fish. The fight is over.

The lines are let back out quickly as the captain seeks to repeat the experience in this hot spot. I'm asked to clean off the deck with the hose. When finished, I sit down on the cooler to document the catch in my notes. But the writing is interrupted almost immediately by two more strikes! The very active landing process is repeated. This time we pull in an aku of about 10 pounds, and a bigger shibi in the 15-pound range. Lahi and I handle these without the involvement of the captain, who continues to navigate amidst a newly arriving pile of birds to starboard.

Pilipo states that we are not far seaward from the area in which a menpachi (*Myripristis spp.* or solderfish) fisherman had died just a few days earlier while night fishing. Pilipo continues on the easterly course for a few minutes but then turns around and heads due west again, hoping to get back into the school.

When asked to move some ice from the fish box to the cooler to ensure better coverage of the growing cache of fish, I notice the aku we just landed has a large chunk missing from its side. Lahi says it looks like a mahimahi bite. When the mate holds up the creature to show Pilipo the hole, the captain winces. The fish is marketable, but the hole means decreased value.

Southbound

It is well after 6:00 p.m. now and the sun is sinking fast. But we continue our westerly course with hopes for more action. After a little while, though, it becomes clear the blitz has ended. Pilipo makes another turn, this time with a little more southerly direction in the bearing. The swell has filled in nicely now; the waves are 6 to 8 feet as measured from the back as they pass by. Because the swell seems to emanate from the north rather than the northwest, however, their size diminishes as we travel south of the headland, which blocks the wave train. Pilipo comments on the situation, noting his amazement of how much smaller it is "een-side den out-side."

Maile Kai is now southbound, its captain and crew fishing along under the subtle pinks and oranges of the setting Hawaiian sun. As we pass the dark rocks, shadows, and precipitous cliffs along the coastline, I remember the legends of ancient Hawaiians and the burial caves here. This was a point of leina a ka ʻuhane, a jumping-off place of spirits bound for the next world. We pass a beautiful beach, then a lush valley, its high green peaks lit with a final glow. Pilipo is focused on the sea rather than sky, however, and says this is the place for kawakawa (*Euthynnus affinis* or wavy-back skipjack fish, a cousin of the aku). Lahi counters, saying, "No, humuhumu" (Humuhumunukunukuapuaʻa or aculeate triggerfish—*Rhinecanthus aculeatus*—the state fish of Hawaiʻi).

Breaking surf resounds in the air here, even though we are still almost a mile offshore. Pilipo must hear it, too, for he mentions this spot is notorious for "ghost waves"—giant swells that refract around the headland to break on shallow spots in the reef.

There is a switch in wind direction, now from the south and fairly fresh. This seems unusual, given the strength of the northeasterly trade winds encountered all afternoon. But such are the tricks of wind around mountainous islands. Some light lingers in the western sky, just enough to assist in initial cleaning up and stowing of certain gear, including the radio and GPS, no longer needed. Pilipo motions me to come closer and says:

> Dis whan tee-pee-cool day fo-ah ahs brah. . . . But da lass strikes good teeng, yeah? Odda-wise da trip not have paid fo-ah da expenses . . . da mahi!
>
> [This has been a typical day for us. The last strikes we had were really fortunate. Otherwise we would have lost the money we invested in the trip. The mahi we caught—really fortunate!]

At just that moment there is a terrific POP! and a loud "z-z-z-z-z-z-z-z-z-z-z-z-z-z-z-z" as the corner outrigger on the starboard side releases and the line rushes out at full speed. "Ho!" cries Lahi, who is on the rod in a second, pumping and reeling. I reel in the other lines as quickly as possible, and a large silver flash some distance astern catches my eye, even in the approaching darkness. Throttling down as he leaves the bridge, the captain asks me to go above and watch the water ahead to look out for other boats while he assists the mate. The autopilot steers as the captain and Lahi gradually wrestle the energetic fish up to the boat. Finally, the mate grabs the leader, his hand partly covered with a fingerless glove, and maneuvers the fish so that Pilipo can reach it with the gaff. The first gaffing attempt fails, but the second is successful and once gaffed, the fish is raised well above the gunwale so it's not bumped back into the water. It's a big ono, over 30 pounds and about 45 inches long. It thrashes wildly on deck until Pilipo covers it with the blanket. The fish takes lots of effort to kill but in the end rests quietly in the large fish box.

Lahi is really excited at this point and says, more to himself than to Pilipo, "We turn around, go again!" But Pilipo says the event was good fortune and not likely to happen again. No matter—Lahi's serious demeanor has been transformed to one of overt happiness. He whistles while cleaning the deck and securing the outriggers for our eventual entry into the harbor.

It's truly dark now, and the captain navigates by memory as much as sight as we slowly make for the channel. We pass the shadowy breakwater some 200 yards off the port side, then turn hard to port and throttle down. The green channel marker light is just ahead. Pilipo hesitates and has a look around before continuing. But there is little swell reaching the mouth of the harbor this evening, and no other vessels are visible.

Pau? Not Yet

Pilipo navigates slowly and carefully through the harbor, making a large arc past the last finger pier before entering his slip. It is a little after 8:00 p.m.

Lahi secures the bow and starboard lines to the dock cleats, and with the gaff, I grab the fixed line on the piling and secure the port stern. The moon is coming up, and the streetlights at the harbor also help us to see.

David is at the dock to greet us with a large Hawaiian teenager Pilipo calls "Sweets." "Hey, Sweets! How-seet bubbah? . . . What you doing to-night brahh?" Pilipo calls out as he continues his breakdown duties. ["Hey, Sweets! How are you doing, kid? What are you up to tonight?"] Standing on the edge of the finger pier, Sweets smiles, first looking down shyly at his feet, then up and over to Pilipo, and replies, "Hey Pee-leepo! . . . Ohhh, we going peeg hahn-ting, you know . . . up mowkah . . . in da moon-light. Go bow en arrow." ["Oh, hello Pilipo! We're going hunting for pigs up in the mountains tonight, in the moonlight. We plan to use bow and arrow methods."]

David says prophetically, "Hey, be care-fool up dey-ah, brah." But Pilipo reminds Sweets of the *real* threat:

> Watch out fo-ah da ate foot Why-inn, bruddah! . . . Peegs no problem, eh?
>
> [Watch out for the 8-foot Hawaiian, kid! The pigs present no problems compared to the 8-foot Hawaiian.]

I know little about this tale of the 8-foot Hawaiian, but from the way everyone talked, I personally don't care to explore the myth in the mountains in the dark! Sweets looks worried for just a moment but then deflects the story, saying something about going with his dogs and that he would have his weapons, too. While there is humor in all of this, there is also seriousness about a midnight hunt under the full moon, and certain comments about pig blood running "tick" [thick] remind me of other folks I have met in my travels; hunting and fishing for food are critically important aspects of life here and in other rural areas of the nation.

But for the moment, Sweets, David, and his friends loiter around the dock, checking out the catch and assisting Pilipo and Lahi with various duties—yet another case of laulima.

Upon arrival on dry land, I shake hands with David, Sweets, and friends, and they smile and treat me well, asking me about the day. David is particularly helpful in assisting the captain and mate, as there is much to be done. Everything must be washed down thoroughly and gear stowed below and locked. The most onerous task is refueling the vessel. This takes much time and effort, and spilled fuel on the boat, dock, and hands must be cleaned with soap and water. The boat is then restarted and the engine revved one last time before being shut down for the night. Finally, the captain and crew load the fish from the cooler and fish box into the fish bag, adding as much ice as the bag will handle. They lift the bag from the boat onto the pier and then onto the iron cart for transport to Pilipo's pickup truck. Extra care on the part of the captain and crew ensures that the cart stays centered on the narrow pier, lest the catch and day's effort be dumped overboard!

Pilipo pushes the fuel barrel up the ramp but lingers for a moment to talk story with Sweets and the others. They discuss the upcoming funeral for the menpachi fisherman who had drowned near the Point. Pilipo and followers are angered that the man's identification and other personal papers were stolen from his truck as family members searched the area for their beloved and his vessel after it was deemed missing. "Dass so cold," said Sweets. ["That's so cold-hearted."] There was also some question about why the vessel sank because the accident occurred during a period of relative calm between swells. There was no clear display of grieving emotion, however. Rather, I got the sense that those present felt that while the event was unfortunate, it was an accepted part of fishing, part of life along a rugged coastline. Some of the young men said they would be going to the service.[2]

At the Auction House

I ask to follow Pilipo to the auction, continuing observation of the captain's already long day. It is 9:00 p.m., leaving only an hour to make it to the auction, which closes at 10:00. We take Lahi to his home, a small one-story unit near the ocean. A group of keiki (kids) comes to the door to greet him. Clearly, he is not alone in this life but rather belongs to a large ʻohana. Given the otherwise subdued manner of our relations to date, I am surprised at the warmth of his farewell to me. He comes over to my car and offers a solid shakka handshake, a big smile, and "Tanksprah." I was touched and excited to have had the opportunity.

We reach the auction house by about 9:45 p.m. A friendly old local Samoan man named Simi sits at a small table in an official-looking uniform and greets Pilipo with a smile, asking how he did this day. "Ahhhhh," says Pilipo, pulling on a pair of black rubber boots at the entrance to the cold, wet fish house, "small

[2]I, too, went to the well-attended service the following Saturday. The fisherman was haole but had lived in the community for some 30 years and was well liked. His wife was pure Hawaiian, from Molokaʻi. About 75 members of her family attended the service, which involved the scattering of ashes at sea. A kupuna from Hālawa Valley on Molokaʻi led the ceremony, asking for permission from the gods to scatter the ashes and asking for blessings from certain winds by performing Kumu Kamakane (a wind call).

kine ah-ku, wahn she-bee, whan mah-hee, en wahn oh-no." ["We caught some little skipjack tuna, one small yellowfin tuna, one mahimahi, and one wahoo."] The captain tells me to pick out a pair of boots from the auction's boot locker and to grab a cart so we can unload the fish. There is no one around to assist, so we put the fish on the scales for weighing.

Simi shuffles some papers and begins recording our catch on a ledger. Pilipo calls out the species as the Samoan man marks down the weight. We then carefully arrange the fish on a pallet for a superficial quality inspection, also leading to marks on a ledger. Pilipo is careful to put the mahi-bitten aku bite-down so that the hole is not readily visible. Simi then gives Pilipo a stack of small, red papers upon which *Maile Kai* is stamped in black letters. These are placed on the larger of the fish and will serve to identify the source of the whole pallet when presented to buyers for bidding in the morning. Just as we finish, a truckload of young fishermen pulls up, minutes before closing time. They load a large, headless marlin and assorted smaller fish on the scales.

Pilipo and I cooperate to wheel the pallet into a freezer in the back of the auction house and use a nearby shovel to cover the fish with ice. I am struck by the level of care Pilipo gives this process, making sure every inch of every fish is covered.

While in the back freezer, Pilipo asks me to share a view of a large big-eye tuna stored in a tank of icy water, to be auctioned on the morrow. Pilipo knows the captain of the vessel that landed the behemoth and looks at the fish wistfully, commenting:

> Brah, dass wahn beeg feesh, eh?, High doll-ah. . . . I know da guy, feesh ad-dah side. . . . Wahn small-boat troll-ah.
>
> [That's a really big fish, isn't it my friend? It will bring a high price. I know the fisherman who caught it. He fishes the other side of the island regularly. He's a small-boat troll fisherman, too.]

The fish will fetch a high price at auction because it is the most desirable of the tunas. It was a really good day for Pilipo's friend, as a fish of that size and quality would bring about $800 to $1,100 based on then-current prices.

I return the boots to the locker and Pilipo has a final word with Simi. A receipt will be sent to Pilipo's home in a couple of weeks indicating the amount paid for the fish at auction. As we stand leaning on his truck getting ready to leave, Pilipo reminds me again that this is a typical day for him and that he plans to fish again tomorrow. He says he will gas up the truck and fuel barrel on the way home, go home and eat, make a lunch, and do whatever else needs doing, probably getting to bed around 1:00 a.m. Given that his day reportedly starts around 3:30 a.m., it seems a challenging lifestyle, at best. But it should be remembered that the fisherman fishes when the weather is good and when the vessel is working. There is "plenny down-time" [plenty of time when the boat isn't at sea].

We shake hands three ways, then part, Pilipo's old pickup rattling off into the back streets of Honolulu. It is almost 11:00 p.m., but I've succeeded in observing and assisting a for-profit fisherman carry out the living of a normal workday, and I sleep well this night.

Analysis

I attempted to contact Pilipo many times over many weeks to determine the value of the fish we landed, finally reaching him three months later. The captain reviewed his files and called me back with the following information:

> Wahn ʻahi, fifteen pounds at whan doll-ah ninetee; seex ah-ku, total seventeen pounds, one-dollah; wahn ah-ku, nine pounds, five doll-ahs, wahn mah-hi, nineteen pounds, five doll-ahs seextee; wahn ono, terdy-wahn pounds, fo-ah ninetee. . . . Dat fo-ah total tree-hunred-foahtee eight eightee, minus ten percent fo-ah da auction. Dat leaves tree-hunred terteen ninetee-two minus wahn hunred foah fuel and ice, leaves two-hunred terteen minus seventy-wahn foah Lahi.
>
> [The one yellowfin tuna weighed 15 pounds and brought $1.90 per pound; the six small skipjack tuna weighed a total of 17 pounds and brought $1.00 per pound; the one big aku weighed 9 pounds and brought $5.00 per pound; the one dolphinfish weighed 19 pounds and brought $5.60 per pound; and the one wahoo weighed 31 pounds and brought $4.90 per pound. . . . That made for a total of $348.80, minus the 10 percent that the auction takes for its services. That leaves $313.92, minus $100 for fuel and ice, which leaves $213 minus $71 for Lahi.]

Thus, over the course of a difficult 20-some hour day, Pilipo earned around $7 an hour. His mate earned under $4 an hour. But Pilipo has indicated that about a third of his profit is put back into the vessel for maintenance. In reality, then, Pilipo earned about $95 profit, or about $4.75 per hour over the course of the long day. This was definitely a bad day in economic terms. Other days in the overall operational cycle are much better. Nevertheless, there is much validity and sincerity in the captain's assertion that "bruddah, we not getting reech out dey-ah!" ["We are not getting rich out there, my friend."]

Using findings from Hamilton and Huffman's (1997) work, it is indeed clear that full-time pelagic small-boat fishermen are not getting rich. According to the authors, the average operation in this fleet expends mean fixed costs of $8,147 and mean per trip expenses of $135. When trip costs are averaged across a mean of 152 trips per year and summed with fixed costs, operators spend an average of $28,667 annually. Fixed costs here include insurance, loan payments, maintenance repairs, gear, and license and registration fees. Trip costs include ice, boat fuel, bait, and truck fuel. Meanwhile, the mean gross revenue from fish sales is reported as $52,948 per boat. Thus, the average boat like Pilipo's earns about $28,667 per year *before* payment of crew (33 percent) and *before* taxes (at least 20 percent). With these figures added into the equation, such fishermen are nearing the poverty level. Small-boat fishermen specializing in hand-line methods offshore the Big Island appeared to be doing somewhat better during the late 1990s, and some have developed innovative methods to further their chances for economic success. But even that group appears increasingly constrained by fuel costs, market conditions, and various other challenges affecting the larger fleet.

In short, full-time small-boat pelagic fishing is hard work over long hours, for low pay, and with considerable financial and bodily risk. In my experience and based on various literature (e.g., McGoodwin 1990), the challenges are common to commercial small-boat operators around the world. Further, given that generation of revenue is dependent on the harvest and distribution of finite resources in a context of increasing regulation and competition, the enterprise is full of uncertainty—surely a psychological burden to participants.

What, then, is the incentive to fish? For many full-time fishermen in Hawai'i, meeting the demands of investment creditors is an important motive. Prospective fishermen willingly save enough to make the down payment on a boat and engine, then must conduct a long-term for-profit operation to pay off the note. Yet it is clear both that an interest in fishing underlies the purchase and that many continue to enjoy the activity despite the pressures to make the payments.

The fact is that many fishermen in Hawai'i report being satisfied with fishing *as a way of life*. Pilipo often receives little financial return for his physical, financial, and emotional investment. But he *enjoys* it. After receiving a lengthy reiterated account of the challenges Pilipo encounters on a daily basis, I put the question of motivation to him directly in two ways. First I asked, "Pilipo, what would you do if you couldn't fish; how would you earn a living?" and then, "Why do you do it? Why do you go fish when it's so difficult?" His reply was as follows:

> Ohhh, brah, [pause] you see what I wen go tru. Ehh-vree-day, brah! En da engine was rahnning when you get on da boat. Dere's mo-ah to da storee brah. You see wahn segment. Dry-dock, dats whe-ah wahn beeg chunk of da finances go, yeah? We go dry dock, so da boat eez ocean safe. [pause] So, brah, you *have* to enjoy eet. You cannot do eet half-heartahlee—nevah survive, eh?
>
> [Brother, you saw what kind of day I had, what I have to endure. Every day is like that! And the engine was running when you got on board. There is a lot more to the story than what you observed. You saw just one segment of what it takes to keep things running. When I have to take the boat out of the water to work on it, that's where a big chunk of my money goes, do you understand? We have to work on the boat constantly so it will be safe for travel at sea. So, my friend, troll fishermen like me *have* to enjoy this way of life. You can't undertake this venture halfheartedly. You would never survive.]

Pilipo enjoys the challenge and meeting it. This is both his account of the situation and my assessment of it. But there is yet another version of the story that can inform understanding in this case, and the preceding pages have provided a glimpse of that—the manner in which Pilipo lives his daily life on the ocean and land, and the way he makes sense of his own actions and those around him. Significantly, Pilipo's admission of enjoying his lifestyle and its challenges was immediately followed by criticism of the market and statements that small-boat fishermen are mistreated there. Thus, while he enjoys meeting the challenges of fishing, and many of these would exist with or without an improved system of marketing as they are an inextricable part of fishing itself, he does not enjoy those external factors that unnecessarily burden him. Of the market, he says:

> Sahm ye-ahs mo bettah den ah-dahs, yeah? You gonna have wahn good yea-ah, I mean catcheen feesh, but might have one bad ye-ah fo-ah da prices, eh? Da quess-chun eez, ah da buy-azz wen playen games? I catch ten large ah-ku, take good care ahv 'em. But da beeg ah-ku boat comes een wit ten towsend pounds. Dey put 'em

right out. Da bidding start up, like two feef-tee. Da buy-ahs buy 'em ahp. Den dey start playeeng games wit ah-wah feesh, push 'em down to wahn eight-ee. But ahwah feesh een bettah shape!

[Some years are better than others, do you understand? You might catch lots of fish one year, but the prices paid for them at market might be bad, see? The question is, are the buyers playing games with us, manipulating us? Consider this. I catch ten large skipjack tuna, and I take good care of them, ice them down quickly. But the big commercial boat comes in to the auction with 10,000 pounds. The auction workers put the fish caught by the big boat operators out for view for bid by the fish buyers, leaving my fish in the back, relatively obscured. The bidding starts at, say, $2.50 per pound. The buyers buy up the 10,000 pounds right away. Then the buyers play price games with the fish that is left, our fish. Even though the fish caught by the small-boat troll fleet is in better shape than that caught by the big boats, they push the price down, down to $1.80.]

Conditions at the market in many ways shape the manner in which Pilipo operates. Some of the pressures have positive effects in that the captain is forced to be as efficient as possible and take good care of his fish. But inasmuch as they result in financial burden, market forces are a serious challenge. Most of the profit from sale of fish accrues to the buyer, to the middleman who typically is not involved in the actual act of fishing. The fisherman himself sees relatively little return. This begs for more detailed analysis of the dynamics between the individual fisherman and the society and economics of the marketplace. It has to be kept in mind that the middleman, the auction owners, and the big-boat operators each must also deal with various challenges to successful business. Part of the problem may well relate to the degree to which seafood prices reflect the full and actual value of seafood, and the willingness of people to pay full value for it. But the focus here is less on the nature of external forces and institutions *per se* and more with the way in which the fisherman deals with those externalities and/or ignores them.

The immediate demands of small-boat commercial fishing engage the captain directly in his personal enterprise. There are no hierarchical layers of authority. Such fishermen typically value the freedom of being their own boss. Moreover, many of the rewards of fishing are immediate and begin as soon as the vessel clears the harbor, or even in anticipation of the freedom of being on the water.

Freedoms and nonpecuniary rewards notwithstanding, the market truly does not offer Pilipo the incentives it might. But, by Pilipo's account, he will not and does not let that get in the way of his lifestyle. In many ways, his life is self-styled *in spite of* the market. Pilipo is an individual working in and through an established economic system, but he is aware of and reactive to that situation. He is intimately aware of economic constraint. He knows even the finest subtleties of social and political interaction in the marketplace. But he has no overt desire (or time) to defeat those forces, to overturn the market through some sort of revolt or, more realistically, to develop a small-boat fishing cooperative, an option he knows has never worked out in Hawai'i. Pilipo loves his way of life, dislikes whatever restricts it, and formulates practical, personal ways to deal with the situation on a daily basis. He understands how to streamline his operation over the long term, but he also knows he doesn't really have a chance at earning extensive profit. So he resigns himself to the immediate rewards of fishing—that is, the freedoms it affords, simply being on the ocean, and the occasional good days at the market.

Pilipo is indeed individualistic and perhaps more so than many of his fellow fishermen—as his interaction with the remora-like captain made clear. Nevertheless, he is not alone in his way of living, and he has not formulated in a vacuum his strategies, techniques, or methods. The captain is at an advanced stage of acquisition of fishing knowledge and experience, but this does not mean he is immune to social aspects of the undertaking. Indeed, at one time he learned from others, and now he imparts knowledge to others. He is, in fact, highly respected, and many at the harbor see him as a kind of fishing icon.

Further, although he may not offer such in his own verbal account, the preceding description reveals that it is, in part, with and through his fellow fishermen that much of his enjoyment of fishing is derived. While his communicative interactions with Lahi are somewhat one-sided, there is an observable if silent camaraderie and sensitivity between captain and mate. The mate invariably knows what to do without prompting from the captain. This makes the captain visibly proud and pleased and his own job that much easier, and he will say as much. Lahi's own abilities to react quickly and effectively indicate acquired skill, awareness, close verbal and nonverbal communication with the captain, and alacrity.

Pilipo also enjoys interaction—at a distance—with his fellow fishermen. He denies the significance of certain radio reports but clearly values others, and he judges all of them. Veteran fishermen and "hard-core" or avid fishermen are given more credence than the novice, or the "weekend warrior."

The social aspects of fishing are made clear in the way fishermen ascribe status to each other. Status cannot be ascribed or achieved in the absence of society, of course, and, in the case of Pilipo, it is clear that many who know him hold him in high esteem. In a place where "fish is currency," Pilipo is the fisherman's fisherman, fishing often and fishing hard, often with success. It is clear, on review of others' accounts of Pilipo and his operation, that he has achieved high status. It remains uncertain, however, whether this is a motive for the fisherman himself to carry forward in the manner he does. Perhaps this question can never be adequately answered, for Pilipo, being a strong-willed individual, would never admit to acting to further his own reputation.

Despite his juxtaposition with and participation in a community of fishermen, the captain does like to fish in solitude. While this makes sense to him from an economic perspective, especially where a school is feeding or where valuable gear is threatened by captains who don't heed the etiquette of leeway, navigating on a wide-open sea is undoubtedly part of what offsets the difficulties of the overall experience. Ostensibly, Pilipo enjoys the physical challenges involved in fishing. But he is not overly masochistic in this respect. His boat is beamier than many, affording stability in rough seas, and he says he likes being comfortable. In reality, Pilipo has a tough disposition, and conditions that are comfortable to him would likely be considered painful to most of the rest of us.

In any case, Pilipo loves the ocean. This is an important factor through which the fisherman partially defeats the external factors that constrain his operation. Otherwise, he might quit fishing, go back to construction work if he could find it, or go on welfare. I don't refer to a kind of tourist appreciation of being on the ocean, wherein the participant engages in whale watching, charter fishing for a day, or other forms of sightseeing at sea. Pilipo has spent much of his life on the ocean in boats. The process of maintaining and operating a fishing vessel, of fishing, and of being on the ocean in general has become, to a certain degree, habitual for him. Yet there is something about life on the open ocean that tends to disrupt the routine, something that is not attainable elsewhere. Fishing is a venue for experiencing that.

There is yet another explanation for Pilipo's persistence in fishing, this requiring some degree of analytical synthesis. I refer to the process and phenomenon of self-identification, in this case, as fisherman. In local parlance, a fisherman who reaches a certain advanced age, a high level of experience, and elevated social status might be called "da mastah" (the master). The term thus describes a person of recognized maritime knowledge and achievement.

The kindly, grey-headed, and bearded Uncle Saul, the local fisherman of many decades, has achieved such status and is revered by young and old alike. Though they need not be fishermen and most certainly may be women, Native Hawaiians call such persons *kupuna,* or revered elders.

Uncle is a navigator par excellence, a person highly knowledgeable of the marine environment, and a seasoned fisherman. Should Pilipo live long enough and continue his career, he, too, may enjoy such title and status. But kupuna do not necessarily work toward becoming recognized as such; rather, such persons behave in a personally sensible manner that is also socially and culturally respectable and valued, and so find themselves in a position of earned respect.

There is thus an inextricable relationship, in this case, between personal behavior and the moral and ethical bounds or norms of local society. In his youth and maturing years, Uncle Saul behaved as he saw fit in keeping with his culture and his own conscience. He dedicated himself to a kind of life on and around the ocean that was appreciated by local society. It is not, therefore, a great conceptual leap to infer that Uncle Saul has developed a strong perception of self and an identity closely related to his successful life as a local mariner and fisherman.

Pilipo is not exactly a gregarious being, but he unavoidably is a social one, and whether he is aware or cares, he is moving toward kupuna status among a society of local fishermen. I have no doubt that Pilipo operates with a strong sense of who he is—a good fisherman and mariner—and that this too is part of his motivation for persisting in and enjoying what will now be a lifelong venture on the ocean.

5/Fishing for Food

Much small-boat fishing in Hawai‘i is conducted with the intent of catching fish to eat. The local term for food and eating, *kaukau* (pronounced "cow-cow"), might be a good way to express the rationale for this brand of fishing. This chapter focuses on the Native Hawaiian fisherman and how he reacts to a relatively recent history of social and economic marginalization by blending adaptive food-gathering strategies with customs developed and practiced over the course of history. For rural Hawaiians especially, fish, shellfish, tako (octopus), limu (seaweed), and upland resources such as pig and taro are critically important to the family diet and for continuity of customary sharing and other significant activities, such as the lū‘au. Using seafood as components of generalized and direct reciprocity systems is also common and important. The resources and traditions are significant, too, for those living in the more populated areas where wild foods are also desired, if harder to come by. Sharing of seafood within and across rural and urban areas is quite common in Hawai‘i.

The term *subsistence* has often been used in reference to hunting, fishing, and gathering activities undertaken by indigenous people around the world. But in modern times, most people undertaking such activities are involved to greater and lesser degrees in the complex societies and economies surrounding them. A tribe or two in the Amazon may still be living in isolation, but this is an exception. Most indigenous peoples are now influenced by concepts and social and economic processes that have arrived from elsewhere. These typically lead to use of a range of modern products and involvement in a cash economy. Even the Inupiat Eskimos in the most distant areas of North America need cash and appreciate many of the things it can buy, and it has been that way for a century or so. Interestingly though, what it often buys them is the tools and materials they need to fish, hunt, and gather! For many indigenous peoples, a desirable use of money is that which enables food gathering and associated cultural practices that have roots in the distant past.

The lifeways and lessons of the past are critically important and deeply valued by Alaska Natives and Native Hawaiians. But the benefits of modernity are also typically valued, and modern life incurs certain demands such as payment of taxes and coverage of health care costs, among many others. The problem is that the old ways of living and the requirements of earning money in the modern setting are not always compatible. In the context of this case study, for example, fishing by boat for consumptive and cultural purposes requires cash and hence, various means for getting it. It is highly significant, if obvious, that for many Native peoples and others who emphasize subsistence fishing activities, participating avidly in that lifestyle necessarily takes away from time potentially spent working a higher–paying, land-based job and accumulating capital—capital that could be used to further subsistence practices and stave off forces that could ultimately constrain those practices. This conundrum is revisited again a bit later in this chapter and the next.

LAWAI‘A: A BRIEF HISTORY

Lawai‘a (fishing) to eat was central to life in Hawai‘i very early on. For example, fishhooks dated to the fourth century have been recovered in conjunction with fish bones and mollusk shells at the Bellows site on O‘ahu (Tuggle et al. 1978). Kirch (1985) suggests that similar findings at Ka Lae may date from the same time period. Fishing and seafood undoubtedly remained central aspects of life for Hawaiians throughout the centuries prior to contact with Europeans. As is documented in many archival sources, dependence on the sea continued throughout subsequent eras as well, and when ancestral lands and social organization were disrupted following contact with Europeans, people used fishing as a means of survival within an imposed economic order.

There have always been people living on the geographic and socioeconomic margins in Hawai‘i. Survival-oriented fishing with relatively little involvement in the cash economy was probably not unusual in rural areas during much of the nineteenth and even the early twentieth centuries. Maly and Maly's (2003) oral histories of fishing experts in the Hawaiian Islands have filled gaps of understanding that would have otherwise remained obscured by time. The work makes clear that Native Hawaiian fishing traditions and ecological knowledge continued to evolve across the Islands even amidst the hegemonic tendencies and capitalist practices of the haoles.

Elderly informants participating in this case study research recalled childhood days in the 1920s and '30s when their kupuna took them fishing. Outboard motors had arrived, the first vertical crankshaft outboard having been invented in 1907 by Ole Evinrude and mass-produced in 1910. These were eventually available for use on small boats in Hawai‘i, although many elderly Native Hawaiian fishermen reportedly didn't desire them. Even at that late date, most Hawaiians reportedly preferred the old ways—the silence of the paddled canoe, the feeding of the ko‘a to attract ‘ōpelu, and use of various ancient methods to catch ‘ahi. Scobie (1949:289) notes similar resistance to new ways, stating that "the Hawaiians still preferred the fishhooks they made themselves rather than those that could be bought."

But the social system that enabled the ahupua‘a system of land use and management and the physical manifestation of traditional knowledge in the form of bone hooks and cordage line was increasingly disrupted. Thus, line from olonā (*Touchardia latifolia*) was rarely used unless it had been saved from days gone by. Abbott (1999) related that while her uncle possessed some cordage made from coconut fiber, he often used butcher string for fishing line.

Sharing and systems of reciprocity involving fish and other foods were and are important adaptive processes for Hawaiians reacting to the social changes following what many recognize as an imperialist invasion by the haoles (e.g., Churchill and Venne 2005). These were also important processes for immigrants struggling to adapt to plantation society. As a mixed society of persons emerged amidst similar economic circumstances during the Plantation era, subsistence activities and sharing of resources fostered the emergence of *local* society.

A propensity for sharing fish and other seafood remains characteristic of Native Hawaiians and other ethnic groups in Hawai'i. Tough economic conditions throughout the 1990s undoubtedly furthered involvement in fishing and gathering shoreline foods. Following a lengthy study in 1994, for instance, Matsuoka and colleagues described the importance of subsistence pursuits and sharing among primarily Native Hawaiian families on Moloka'i:

> Without subsistence as a major means for providing food, Moloka'i families would be in a dire situation. Subsistence provides families with the essential resources that compensate for low incomes and a means for obtaining food items that may [otherwise] be prohibitively costly. . . . This dependency on subsistence resources is even more paramount when examined against the backdrop of relatively low income levels. . . . Close to half of the sample [n = 241] made less than $20,000 annually. . . . Among the Hawaiian families surveyed, 38 percent of all food consumed is acquired through subsistence activities . . . 51 percent of respondents said they fished throughout the year . . . 42 percent troll fished. . . . (Matsuoka et. al 1994:5, 46)

Consumptive-oriented hunting and fishing activities and sharing of the resources are common integrating factors in the 'ohana setting across the Islands. These are enacted on both a regular basis and during special periods or events, such as the baby lū'au, graduations, weddings, funerals, and other social occasions. When a baby reaches its first birthday, local families celebrate the baby lū'au, a tradition that lingers from a time not long ago when infant mortality was much higher than today.

Earlier I noted statistically significant evidence of relationships between fishing for ceremonial purposes and receiving fish caught by others, suggesting a network of fish-specific reciprocity. Fishermen frequently save some of their catch in anticipation of such events or make trips specifically for the purpose of catching fish to eat and share at 'ohana gatherings. Sharing fish may also be accompanied by certain rituals. Native Hawaiian fishermen will sometimes make offerings at the heiau, as was repeatedly observed at a remote location in Ka'u District on Hawai'i. It is also customary for fishermen to share the first big catch of the season.

Fish may be shared with strangers as well, perhaps simply as part of good-natured disposition and aloha. An elderly local haole fisherman born on Hawai'i

Island told me stories of times past and the perennial "big heart" of the Native Hawaiian:

> Plenny beeg haht, dose old Why-ins, yeah? Dey get plenny haht. I fought, oh how we fought each ahh-dah. Dey still call me how-lee boy, you know. But when dey love you, ohhh . . . dey geev you evrie-ting brah—da shirt right off de-ah backs. . . . Dey bring feesh ovah, take care of *you* brah! (Fieldnotes, Kona Coast, Spring 1999)
>
> [Those old Hawaiians have really big hearts, do you understand? I fought with them during my youth. Oh how we fought until I established myself. They still call me haole boy, you know! But when they accept you—oh, they give you everything, my friend—the shirts right off their backs! They bring you fish; they take care of *you,* brother!]

I experienced more directly the tendency toward sharing and aloha among Native Hawaiians as a friend and I camped at remote Miloli'i along the Nā Pali Coast of Kaua'i. A trio of young Hawaiian men seemed at times to circle our camp. They would repeatedly glance over, then seeing us notice them, look back to the ground or up at the sky as they walked or played on the beach and under the cliffs under the warm summer sun. On the second day, the circling tightened a bit, and the glancing increased until finally they made their way over to talk with us. They were very shy but wanted to share some fish they had speared on the reef and had stored in their coolers. I heartily agreed to the offer and asked if they would like some 'opihi (limpets) in return. They declined but told me to wait, that they would be right back. They returned smiling proudly some minutes later with a plastic bag full of manini (*Acanthurus sandvicensis*), āholehole (*Kulia sandvicensis*), and ice. I thankfully stored the fish for later, and we talked story for some time about the Nā Pali coast, the cliffs and birds overhead, the goats that had visited the camp that morning, the ancient ali'i canoe burial on the hill above us, and other things Hawaiian.

Scene from a combination troll and spear trip offshore the Big Island, 1998

Based on my findings about the ubiquity of sharing fish in Hawai'i and particularly high rates of sharing on the Big Island, and Hamilton and Huffman's (1997) findings of significantly lower household income among fishermen on the Big Island, I posit that a flexible Hawaiian-style approach to subsistence-oriented fishing is quite common here. Less emphasis is placed on dedicated involvement in the wage economy and much more in an informal one. Fishermen need cash, of course, but they often put the money earned from fishing and other sources back into the fishing operation. I provide an example of how this approach works in the following case study and examine its implications in a concluding analysis.

THE VILLAGE TRIP

The fishing trip always begins with an idea. In this case, my own idea was fishing not to catch fish really but to collect information about the process. On the other hand, the captain and confidante, Kalani (pronounced kah-lah-nee), wanted to go fishing to catch fish—that could be determined without even asking him. I was allowed to go along. But beyond that, I cannot tell you much. I can't tell you if Kalani wanted to go fishing to catch fish to eat, or to catch fish to sell, or to catch fish for fun. In this case, I don't think Kalani knew—from the outset, during the trip, or even after the fish was caught—precisely why he was going fishing. As it was for his father and perhaps his father's father, fishing simply is what he does and loves to do.

The trip described chronologically in the following pages is one of many thousands for Kalani, who reports having fished as a child and on a regular basis throughout his life to his then-present age in his late forties. Kalani says he loves the idea of being able to go out for a couple of hours to "catch fish for lunch." Yet, depending on market prices, size of catch, and ease of travel, Kalani may at times sell his fish to markets in town for pocket money or to pay bills or buy gas for his next trip. He sometimes trades fish for various goods and services and dries or smokes them for future consumption. Fish are also given away, ritually or casually, and may be caught intentionally for consumption at specific family or community functions. This case is an excellent example of the fluid and *ad hoc* mixture of reasons for and outcomes of fishing Hawaiian-style.

The "Plan"

I'd met Kalani previously at a regional fisheries management meeting and later talked with him by phone, each time indicating an interest in going fishing. I then called him on a Sunday night in April 1998. This led to his indicating a continued interest in taking me out on the water. During a call a week later, Kalani told me he had been fishing alone all week but had been catching some ono and could use a hand landing the fish. The following Monday was not possible, however, because he had to travel to town to get some supplies and pay some bills. I was told to call him back Monday night and that we might go on Tuesday. Our conversation Monday night led to a somewhat casual arrangement with no final agreement about the exact time for meeting Tuesday morning.

I was working in another village on the southeast coast and worried about getting down early to meet Kalani in his own village, which is rather isolated in geographic terms. Residents must travel many miles to shop for supplies in the nearest towns, requiring a drive of at least an hour, depending on road and weather conditions. Nevertheless, I was prepared to arrive as soon as a meeting could be arranged—if, that was, he would commit to a set time. Our conversation to arrange the trip went as follows:

Kalani: Yeah, yeah, try come, we mess around, go fo-ah some ono . . . ‘ōpelu maybe. [Yes, yes, try to come down. We'll go out fishing for some wahoo, or maybe some ‘ōpelu.]

Me: Sounds good. About what time should I come down?

Kalani: Mo-ah bettah come early brah . . . try get on 'em. . . . We get out, mess around, go ko‘a, lie dat. [It would be better if you came early, so we can get out there and get started. . . . We'll go mess around, maybe fish the ko‘a, perhaps do something like that.]

Me: So about seven, how is that?

Kalani: Yeah, seven, maybe try go early, eh? . . . We go. [Yeah, maybe around seven o'clock, [but] let's try to go early, got it? We'll go!]

Me: [sensing he was ready to hang up] Okay, so earlier, I'll be there. . . . Oh, where should I meet you?

Kalani: You know . . . where eez da gas pump. . . . Meet you day-ah. [I will meet you at the gas pump.]

Me: Okay, mahalo, thanks.

I reckon Kalani's seeming unwillingness to identify a specific time for departure (other than "early") is related to a sort of island-style culture of "whenevahs," that is, the notion of "Island" or "Hawaiian" time in which being late or relatively unconcerned about the wristwatch and its demands is characteristic. Perhaps it is also courteous concern for me, a visitor, having to get up too early. But I also figure that, being a fisherman, he would actually be ready to go at or before first light. Toward that end, I resolve to get up about 5:10 a.m. with the intent of getting to the village before daybreak at 6:00, just to be sure. Traveling first down the highway, then slowly along the treacherous lower road to the rural village, I disregard the notion of Hawaiian time and, like the haole I was raised to be, worry about being late.

Waiting

5:50 a.m. Sitting on the lava rock wall near the shoreline, I breathe the morning air and wait for dawn. The morning chill slowly departs as the sun ascends the horizon, and a light offshore breeze carries the sweet scent of pua keni keni (*Fagraea berteriana*). The sky is scattered with only high-level cirrus, though a small area of thicker cumulus hovers far to the north. The ocean surface is fairly glassy, but a darker, more textured surface indicates stronger winds toward the horizon.

The little village is peaceful this early morning. Birds sing, stray cats flee an old woman walking her dog in the early light, and the light wind rustles the lau (leaves) of the many coconut palms (*Cocos nucifera*) lining the narrow macadam lane.

6:09 a.m. I find the small northwest swell swashing along the shore mesmerizing, particularly in my still-sleepy state. Suddenly I realize that someone has beaten us to the fishing grounds. A small, weather-beaten vessel with small forward cabin emerges from beyond a point of land to the north, roughly one-half mile from shore. The captain is trolling with four rods.

The sound of a truck brings back awareness of land, but it's not Kalani. Another fisherman in a large, shiny, four-wheel-drive pickup with oversize tires approaches and gives "one shakka" as he rides by.[1] The man tows a 16-foot trailer with a long tongue extension for easy negotiation at the launch ramp. The ramp is quite close to the gas pump in front of Kalani's house. I learn later that the pump is used by Kalani's 'ohana and those who have made arrangements for payment. The truck pulls into an empty lot and then slowly backs up to the boat ramp, far enough so as to immerse the boat. The ramp is actually a natural feature of the shoreline, and the tiny bay that constitutes the launch area is very small, no more than 8 feet across at its widest point, perhaps 12 feet long, and no more than 3 feet deep at low tide.

Another Hawaiian in an old, beat-up station wagon pulls up behind the truck to assist in the launch after stopping to talk to the woman walking her dog. In contrast to the shiny new truck, the vessel is well-used—an aged custom-built 16-foot tub with cuddy cabin and weathered 25 horsepower Mercury engine. The boat is released from the trailer winch, then held in place by the assistant while the driver parks the truck and trailer. In this case, the truck is parked immediately adjacent to the ramp, suggesting the men are local residents with no fear of reprimand for parking so conveniently close to the launch area. The captain boards the boat gracefully and then skillfully and quickly backs the boat out into slightly deeper water. He turns the craft around, navigates a tiny pass in the reef, and is gone, heading off at about 210 degrees. A turn back to the north takes the vessel past the little headland, out of my field of vision. Meanwhile, the driver of the wagon heads off to parts unknown, his cooperative effort temporarily complete.

6:25 a.m. The school bus arrives to pick up kids waiting near the church about 200 yards south of the launch area. A tattered old sign near the bus stop reads "All Stray Pigs Will Be Seized on or after June 21, 1991." The bus driver waves to me on his way back out, beginning the journey back up the dangerous mountain road with his precious cargo of fifteen students.

Just about this time, the vessel I spotted earlier becomes visible as it loops back to the north, ostensibly making some sort of local trolling circuit. The

[1]Pronounced "shah-kah," this commonly used gesture involves elevating the thumb and pinky finger while tilting the hand back and forth sideways on a horizontal axis. The meaning is specific to Hawaii but varies by context. In this case, it was used like a "thumbs-up" might be used on the Continent. But there is more to it, and while living in Hawaii enables one to intuit its various meanings by context, adequate description defies me. It's like "da kine," eh?

vessel that just departed reappears not long after, seemingly on the same general circular route, not far from shore.

6:50 a.m. What I eventually learn is that the yard, house, and shed that appear to be someone's large repository for "all kine stahff" just behind the launch area are actually Kalani's. There are many old trailers, boats parts, engines, burned-out cars, and miscellaneous items in the yard. I am later told by another Hawaiian fisherman that the items are available not only for Kalani, but also for others in the community. I am reminded of my late best friend's yard. What was a bunch of junk to his frustrated wife was actually highly functional equipment to my bruddah. But it defied his ability to adequately store and organize—anchors, chains, floats, nets, various lines, rigs, blocks, and so forth. This seems to be the situation in Kalani's yard, which also harbors a good-sized boat in a state of disrepair, two smaller canvas-covered boats, and an unlocked pickup truck. Two large transport trucks and two derelict mobile-home–style trailers with letters and logos advertising hauling and water supply companies also rest in the yard, speaking to the fisherman's history of occupational plurality. A wooden pole carved into a fierce Hawaiian warrior god marks the entrance to Kalani's rocky driveway, suggesting "kapu" to those who might transgress his trust.

6:58 a.m. Another truck approaches. It is Kalani, finally, and he smiles while pulling into the drive. He wastes no time and backs right up to his trailered vessel. I walk over to help him attach the hitch to the truck. Even though the launch ramp is only about 60 yards away across the lane, the vessel is far too heavy to move without a truck. At least two other families here have safe moorage fronting their residences, but Kalani doesn't, and like the majority of other residents in the area, he must use the tiny launch ramp. The village is at the base of a large ahupuaʻa, and residents of the mauka portion often come down to use the ramp. As in days past, there is still semblance of mutually beneficial economic relations between residents living in the upland and makai portions of this area.

The boat trailer is old and rusty, but because it doesn't have to go far, it does the job just fine. Kalani owns a number of trucks but uses an old rig with rather bald tires to tow the trailer around. We must apply considerable force to coax the trailer onto the hitch ball. Both of us struggle and then finally succeed. The trailer seat—a small but sturdy wooden stand that holds the trailer and boat upright—is kicked out of the way.

7:05 a.m. I hop onto the bed of the pickup. Kalani looks through the open rear window to ask how long I've been waiting. I tell him it's been about an hour but no worry. He then confirms what I suspect, that he usually leaves around daybreak but thought that *I* would end up arriving later! From the perspective of seeking to catch fish, the outcome of this communication gap proves to be an important aspect of our trip, as described later on.

Getting Ready

Fishing trips universally require some forethought and preparation. But making ready often is necessarily "spur of the moment" for fishermen such as Kalani. He tends to decide to fish, or not, at the last moment, based on ever-changing conditions of sea and sky, and reports from his peers. For those who fish regularly, this uncertainty of timing results in some degree of ongoing preparedness so that when the proper conditions present themselves, the trip can be initiated quickly. Gear is typically stored in an accessible place, the vessel and motor are kept ready, and trailers are backed into their parking places, ready for quick hookup to the truck and transport to the launching site when the time is right. I want to make a comparison with surfing because the avid surfer is always ready to go when the various conditions of ocean and climate come together to produce good surf. But it's not quite the same. Surfing big waves calls for physical conditioning and the right board, but the activity requires relatively little preparation in terms of gear. Preparation to fish, on the other hand, requires extensive preparation of gear, vessel, engine, and other components. This ongoing work can be quite involved, with serious implications for safety and success.

Kalani goes into his shed to fill a large plastic trash bag with ice for the cooler and to fetch the rods and reels for placement in the vessel's rod holders. Although he has some personal freezer space for ice, he states that local fishing families would benefit from some sort of community facility for proper storage of fish. He says an ice machine, storage facility, and refrigerated truck would reduce the number of trips to town to market fish, thereby increasing the commercial viability of local fishing operations. The captain also grabs a six-pack of soda and some chips for the trip—clearly not to be an overnighter!

The Equipment

Kalani's current vessel of use is an all-fiberglass 16-foot double-vee whaler design with center console mounted on the forward third of the boat. It is powered by a stern-mounted 70-horsepower outboard. This boat replaced his larger rig after the failure of one of its twin 90-horse engines. Kalani plans to repair it himself at some undetermined point in time. The smaller vessel has two side-mounted "shotguns," or swiveling rod holders that hold short boat rods and 12/0 reels, and two stern mounted reel holders that hold two 10/0 reels.

Kalani doesn't appear overly concerned about organization of lures and rigs. Two old plastic containers without lids hold various lures with plastic skirts amidst old seawater and fish scales. A small tackle box holds various other fishing items common to most small fishing boats—pliers, knife, leader line, swivels, weights, some bandages, and so forth. Expensive or even rudimentary electronics do not seem Kalani's priority either. There is no depth finder, GPS, EPIRB, or even a chart or compass on board. There is a CB radio with antenna, but this is not turned on until we are halfway through the trip. The tachometer is not operational. Kalani knows these waters well and position locating and fish finding are internal processes, at least in the nearshore waters.

At about 7 feet by 3 feet, the homemade fiberglass fish box is quite large, indicative of the size of the bigger fish caught in these waters. Two standard 12 1/2-gallon red plastic fuel tanks with pump ball set-ups fuel the engines. Kalani is already gassed up for this trip, so the cost of the fuel is unclear. Early in the previous day, however, I watched a fisherman in Hilo pump 42 gallons worth of regular grade gas into his inboard tanks for a total cost of $71.50; at that rate, Kalani filled his tanks for about $42 in 1998. [Again, this price will nearly triple a few years later.]

At one point during the day, I hear Kalani respond to a friend who asks why he wasn't going offshore for ʻahi. Kalani relates that the compression of one of the outboard's cylinders is low and that it can't be trusted for a long trip "outside." Indicative of his independent nature, however, Kalani tells his friend that he is going to rebuild the motor before the season gets started. The captain says real ʻahi season is right around the corner, beginning in May, and that "evree-bah-dee drop wat dey do-eeng fo-ah go feesh ah-hee." ["Everybody will drop whatever they're doing to go fishing when the ʻahi show up."] I assume the big fish will be closer to shore during peak season.

Underway

7:07 a.m. We pull over to the launch ramp and back in. I walk on the trailer tongue above the slippery bottom, ready to crank on the winch when the trailer and vessel are deep enough. I crank a turn to unhook the bowline and then get into the water to hold the vessel while Kalani parks the truck. He boards the vessel as I hold it steady in the breeze, and with the hydraulic control, he lets the motor down and then turns the engine right over—no problems. I slip a little while boarding and lose my "rubbah sleep-ah" but then retrieve it quickly. Kalani backs us up deftly, keeping the prop elevated to negotiate the shallow channel. We maneuver through a few waves and then accelerate, heading west.

Quick to Fish

Immediately beyond the zone of breakers along the fringe reef, not more than 120 yards from land, Kalani leaves the wheel to attach the lures and let out the line. We continue to travel west at about 8 knots. I start to take the wheel but see that the vessel generally keeps its course, and when it strays, Kalani steers manually by grasping and moving the outboard motor itself. The side-mount rigs are quickly let out to about 80 yards. The stern-mounted lines are then let out a shorter distance, about 50 yards. For ono, Kalani uses a standard local lure, in this case an orange-headed lure about 4 inches long, with multicolored plastic skirt.

7:19 a.m. Kalani returns to the wheel and alters course to a more southerly direction along what I later learn is the long koʻa, a feature that has long been the focus of local fishermen. There are, in fact, various koʻa in the area. This one is productive for ʻōpelu, the mainstay of the local diet in antiquity. The reef also is attractive to migrating ʻahi and so is a popular trolling area for local fishermen and visitors aware of its location. It runs parallel to the coast just south of the village and about three-quarters of a mile offshore for a distance of about a mile. In days past, ʻōpelu were "trained" to come to such koʻa as residents fed them with a mash of taro, pumpkin, and other vegetable matter. Modern commercial vessels were at the center of controversy at the time of this research because some captains were using chop-chop (fish parts) rather than vegetables to attract ʻōpelu to the koʻa. Some fishermen argue the use of chop-chop brings predators and so makes the fish more skittish and difficult to catch.

There is only a light surface chop from the light southeasterlies, and we run "downhill" ahead of the northwesterly swell. Not minutes into this new course, *we have a strike!* It's not a vicious one, however, and at first Kalani is not even sure a fish is on the line. It is only his constant visual check on the lines that reveals something has happened. "Wahn feesh ahn" says Kalani in a somewhat louder pitch than his usual softly spoken tone, "slow eet down." Given that activity on the small vessel occurs at relatively close quarters, I am already at the wheel and throttle and slow us down slightly so as to facilitate easier reeling in and gaffing of the fish. Even though the fish was caught on the portside stern reel, our positioning has made the starboard side the lee side—more suitable for dealing with the fish as the current pulls the fish and line away from the boat and possible entanglement with the propeller. Thus, the fish is reeled in quickly to the starboard side. A quick rush to the surface reveals that it's an ono.

Once the reeling is nearly complete, Kalani's fingerless glove gives a better grip as he pulls the fish close to the surface by the leader. He asks first for the gaff, with which he quickly and strategically spits the fish under the gill; and then, as it struggles, the bat, with which he will stun the creature. Meanwhile, I attempt to slow us down further but throttle down too quickly, and the engine sputters, then stalls, and we are no longer under power. This is a mistake, of course, and I try to restart but there's a lot happening at once—swell, wind, captain, fish, hook. I try to keep my wits about me and decide that getting the fish in the fish box is the current priority—if, that is, I can find the bat in the rocking boat and get it to Kalani! I fumble a bit, then pass the bat to him, whereupon the fish is dispatched and brought on board. It is "small kine," but its teeth are sharp and I'm warned by a caring captain. Into the fish box it goes. Kalani shows me the trick to the ignition—I was not fully in neutral as I thought. He restarts the motor and we're back underway on the same southerly course.

Interaction on the "High Seas"

7:33 a.m. We continue trolling along the same course and eventually catch up with the early-rising captain. The vessel stays well outside as we catch up. Then, within the last 250 yards, it begins to drift across our path toward land, eventually crossing in front of us. This seemingly elevates the ire of Kalani, who raises his hand and makes a kind of angry "get out of my way" gesture, beckoning the vessel to stay outside toward the open sea. He grumbles about getting "cut off." The fisherman in the other vessel returns the hand motions with equal vigor, signaling to Kalani to "get away." This grumbling and these motions continue for about twenty seconds, and I wonder what might happen next. But I suddenly realize that there were other signals being transmitted and that the anger is feigned. Kalani holds up one finger (not the third), indicating his single fish caught, while the other fishermen holds up four, indicating *his* success. It becomes clear that they are actually friends, and they smile at each other as we overtake the older vessel. What at first seemed to be a miscalculation in course or flagrant violation of etiquette actually turned out to be a well-timed maneuver to let us pass as the other captain kept his lines over the narrow ko'a.

We continue in a southerly direction. The other captain follows for a bit and then turns around. We are alone on the water for about twenty minutes. Eventually, yet another vessel is encountered. Kalani is surprised to see someone fishing so far south. The boat is piloted by some young Hawaiian men from a village about five miles north. "Dey good keeds," Kalani says, noting also that they really go at their fishing full bore, further evinced by the expensive twin engines on their stern. We pass fairly closely as they head back north. As we hold our course, Kalani relates that we're after ono along the 40-fathom ledge, which, in this area, ranges from about a mile out to almost within a stone's throw of the cliff-lined shoreline—quite a rapid drop-off.

We also pass a large commercial dive charter vessel anchored in a blue-green bay. There is nobody visible on the 60-foot, high-tech catamaran—perhaps they're still sleeping. This sighting elicits Kalani's perspective that there is too much commercial activity in the area. Captains of smaller commercial dive vessels were chased away from these waters by local fishermen earlier in the decade because it was believed they were overharvesting certain reef fish species for aquarium collectors. Kalani says that the operators of the charter dive vessel we now pass advocate more of a "look but don't touch" operation and are therefore more tolerable than those who would harvest what are seen as precious local resources.

Kalani usually fishes with his youngest son, who reportedly likes to fish as much as his father does. His oldest son is academically inclined and attends college on the Continent. His daughter is bound for Kamehameha School, the Native Hawaiian–only school on O'ahu. My perception of fishing with Kalani is that he is an even-tempered man with great knowledge of fishing and the sea. He would be a good teacher of fishing and life. His demeanor is such that quick reaction to his softly spoken commands makes for success.

Into the Glassy Zone

8:15 a.m. We round Kaupō Point (pseudonym) some nine miles south of the village, heading in a more southeasterly direction toward a triangular pu'u (hill). I am struck by the placid beauty of the ocean and surrounding landscape here. Kalani says that the water south of Kaupō is usually very rough. The area is called "no-man's land" because on most days the collision of brisk trade winds and currents makes for choppy conditions. But the surface is unusually calm today. Kalani claims that days like these are rare, and he repeatedly states his regret at not having brought bottom-fishing gear. He said that he would have cut up the ono for bait had he brought his bottom gear, though I interpret this to mean that he would have used its less palatable parts for cut bait.

We circle around once and then start heading back north, retracing the original course in the other direction. Kalani stays close to land throughout this part of the voyage, and readily visible physical features along the shoreline continually inform him of our location above certain fishing spots. Kalani, in turn, occasionally informs me. Only the cement foundation of an old lighthouse remains at Kaupō. The captain reports that the structure itself was swept away during a particularly large southerly swell some years back.

Some Grumblings and a New Strategy

8:33 a.m. The wind has picked up a bit, and the surface is a bit more chaotic than during our earlier passage. The wind is to stern, but we are now running into the little swell, and the combination makes for a somewhat rougher ride. The fishing has required patience since our initial strike, and there are the beginnings of grumblings from Kalani, who says quietly, "Dis lousy." We open sodas and eat some chips while looking for birds. These are few and far between, and Kalani thinks aloud that it is significant and unusual that the birds we *do* see are headed south rather than north. The captain mentions the lack of other positive signs as well. Referring to our target of ono he says, "No see 'em jump o-ah nah-teeng, brah. . . . Usually see 'em jump, yeah?"

Seeking a potential remedy to our relative lack of good luck, Kalani begins to head more directly into the open sea, charting a northwesterly course toward "da buoy." The wind and seas increase as we head out to sea into the teeth of a strengthening breeze. Mariners, surfers, paddlers, and others who appreciate smooth surface waters often notice the disruption of these conditions as the morning progresses. The land warms as the sun rises, forcing air aloft. This is replaced by cooler seaborne air rushing landward—the sea breeze effect. This is most noticeable in Hawai'i when the trade winds are slack. The southerly cant to this breeze is unusual, and Kalani remarks that there must be some sort of storm at sea that is influencing its direction. I later discover that he's right—a strong, early season tropical low-pressure system had formed that day northeast of the Hawaiian chain. There is growing cloudiness to our north, and Kalani remarks that the clouds hold rain and that Maui would be getting wet this day—a point also borne out by investigation.

I ask the captain about how he gathers information regarding impending weather. He doesn't own a weather radio, and though his CB radio has a weather band, he indicates it gets little use. He says he watches the weather report on the evening news on the television and looks at the sea and sky. I find his mention of the news interesting because I know he cannot always use a television as there is no electrical service in the village, only solar power, and this is not entirely reliable. He says he won't buy a computer because he feels it may further stress his already overburdened power system.

9:00 a.m. The buoy, a small yellow dot in the distance, is occasionally visible beyond the growing sea and swell. But it grows larger as the minutes pass. As we move farther offshore, the sea becomes a darker hue of blue, now almost indigo. It is very deep here. Eventually we reach the FAD, a 15-foot-tall buoy complete with bird on top. We make two broad circles, trolling unsuccessfully all the while. Kalani's attitude worsens with each passing mile and lack of strikes, and he decides to turn back toward the village, roughly four miles to the northeast.

Back to Da Ko'a

Our forward speed rhythmically increases and then diminishes as the swells roll under and past the small vessel. They pick us up, and we surf along quickly with a feeling of reduced gravity, slowing again as we're deposited in the trough. This calls for constant manipulation of the throttle in an attempt to maintain a somewhat consistent trolling speed. Two lines tangle at one point on the way in, and we stop to free the mess by reeling in both lines simultaneously, then letting them back out separately and carefully.

9:45 a.m. Kalani continues to gauge our position by observing landmarks, eventually announcing that we are back at the ko'a. He steers parallel with a headland to the south, and a few degrees north of the old village site called Napua (pseudonym). Kalani's distant family roots are in Napua; the area was home to many Hawaiians as late as the 1870s. Lava flow and isolation eventually led to its decline as a popular place to live, though the tin roof of an old house was still visible this day against the backdrop of the massive western flank of Mauna Loa.

Kalani slows a little to begin a methodical troll along the ko'a. This continues for about three miles. As we travel, he speaks of the historical importance of the reef:

> Dis same ko'a kept [the village] go-een foah many yeahs, eh? . . . In da sum-mah eet's 'ōpelu. . . . Even een ween-tah . . . get ah-hee too, even een ween-tah.
>
> [This same reef and its resources kept our village going for many years. In the summer we catch 'ōpelu here, but even in winter it's productive and sometimes we can catch tuna here—even in the winter.]

It was during this part of the trip that the captain told me something of his three years in Vietnam and of other personal experiences, including some success as a heavy machinery operator and at various entrepreneurial efforts over the years. He talked about the local lifestyle, too, and the importance that many local residents place on living in this rural area. Hunting for boar and goat in the uplands and gathering 'opihi and limu along the shoreline are important activities for residents. These supplement the typical household diet of fish and store-bought goods. The shoreline is very rugged here, and it has been difficult thus far for outsiders to reach and overexploit shoreline resources. But the area is not without its pressures. As previously noted, resources in the nearshore waters have been contested, and developers have sought to build large resorts in the area.

Kalani says he feels strongly about preserving his way of life. Speaking in reference to the efforts of an investor to develop a large resort complex near Kaupō Point in the 1980s, the fisherman says:

> We still wahn small village, eh?. . . Dey-ahs not much competeeshun—yet. But tings gonna change, you know. Change comeen he-ah, too, eh? If we nehvah fought da resort, would be his-trie, brah. Oh, it was big time bool-sheet, brah. Dey don't understand us . . . don't understand da life he-ah.
>
> [We're stilling living in a small, traditional setting, do you understand? There is not much competition to disrupt our way of life—not yet. But change is imminent, even here. If we hadn't fought the resort development, the village would gone. It was a big battle to stop them. The developers, the outside world, don't understand why we value this way of life.]

According to Kalani, the resort project failed largely due to a concerted local effort to stop it. This involved the efforts of those vocal residents who, as Kalani put it, weren't "bought" by the developer. This conversation further elicited the basic problem I review in this case study. Some local people wanted the resort for the jobs it might bring, whereas others passionately wanted to keep it out. The traditional lifestyle was preserved, and the cultural lives of residents were richer for it, though nothing was gained in purely economic terms. But part of the argument against the development involved questions about what locals might have really gained in economic terms in the long term anyway because it is often the case that the higher-paying positions at Hawai'i resorts are held by haoles (see Adler and Adler 2004).

The fisherman reports other threats to his way of life, not all entirely imposed, as he sees it, from without. For instance, he worries that the productive waters here may eventually be overrun with commercial-oriented local fishermen and aquarium reef-fishing collectors from elsewhere around the region. Kalani desires some sort of regulatory structure that would prioritize the rights of village-based fishermen to local resources whether they are used for commercial, subsistence, or other purposes. His perspective is that village residents operate with a self-limiting conservation ethic that is based on localized norms and customs, and that captains from other areas do not necessarily recognize these and therefore threaten local resources.

To the Ramp

Eventually we near the village, with only the lonely ono in the fish box. Kalani reiterates his opinion that this was a lousy trip, not because of our tactics but because the fish just weren't out there. He says with visible frustration, "No see 'em feed oah nah-ting," and relates his now-false prediction that we would do well this day, especially given unusual wind and the lunar phase—the recent arrival of a new moon. But then, with some degree of resignation in his voice, he says "Ahhh, dat's fishing, yeah?"

We slow down and proceed just past the channel entrance to little Leilani Bay (pseudonym), turning our bow back into the now-blustery southeast wind. This provides some control against lateral movement as we begin to enter the tricky channel. We quickly reel in the lines and proceed slowly into the harbor, keeping an eye astern for following swells and off the bow for coral heads. Kalani comments that the tide is *very* low due to the new phase of the moon. Sure enough, we have a good bump on the way in as a swell picks up the little boat and lays it into a shallow spot. There is no damage, however, only a little ruffling of nerves.

10:20 a.m. Kalani maneuvers into the channel and with a short burst of throttle in reverse, holds us off the rocks. The trip is over. We have traveled roughly twenty-two miles in just over three hours. We load the vessel onto the trailer and park the truck with trailer attached in Kalani's front yard.

We take some pictures of the ono to accompany my notes, chasing away Kalani's cat, who wants some of the fish. Kalani reckons the fish weighs about

20 pounds. He spends five minutes washing off the boat and another five or so storing his gear—a relatively quick period of post-trip involvement! This is facilitated by the fact that his yard is just feet from the ramp and ocean, the fuel tank is immediately adjacent, and his gear and refrigerator are steps from the truck and trailer.

I stand next to the captain without speaking for a moment and then thank him. Kalani pauses for a moment, expresses his regrets for a "lousy" trip, and invites me over to his other house for kaukau.

Da Bruddahs and Da Feesh

We drive over in my rental truck, so Kalani can leave his attached to the trailer, making tomorrow's trip that much easier. We pass the vessel I witnessed entering the water at daybreak, parked on its trailer in a driveway. There are four men hanging around, including the captain and the station wagon driver who assisted his launch. The Hawaiians shout out to Kalani as we pass. They are aware that he is in my truck; this is a small village where the locals seem to know everything about everything almost before it happens. Kalani asks me to stop and back up.

They talk story. Their language is more difficult to understand than is Kalani's. It seems this is a pure version of pidgin not used in conversation with haole guests. I cannot accurately recreate the conversation but can relate the meaning of what was said. In essence, the other men caught three ono, slightly larger than ours, and an ʻahi in the 40-pound range. The men are getting ready to drive to town to sell the fish to a restaurant and ask Kalani if they should take his, too, with his share of the profit to be awarded upon their return. Kalani's reply is in the affirmative and reveals trust in his fellows: "Ees in da back, in da feesh box." He then jokingly tells them to make sure they weigh it out properly. Kalani tells me the ʻahi they caught is "beeg bucks, brah—terty to foahty pound da kine breeng 'em 250 dah-lahs"—over $6.00 a pound. There is mention that another restaurant up the road would likely take one of the ono for the lunch menu, but they are not yet sure which fish would go. Kalani warns that ono prices are down, but the men indicate that the trip to town to sell the ʻahi is worth the effort, and they will sell Kalani's ono, too, while there.

Interestingly, when Kalani asks the men when and where they caught their fish, they reply that they had their luck around Mailehana (pseudonym), the point of land opposite the course we set out on but not too distant from where we caught our ono. Kalani remarks regretfully that maybe he should have gone that way instead of to the south as we did. Of significance, the fishermen say they caught all of their fish in the first hour of their trip—the hour during which I waited for Kalani to show up and the same hour he waited for me at his house, anticipating my late arrival! Because we caught our fish during the initial part of our trip, it seems we may have chanced upon the tail end of a bite. I can tell this vexes him a little, and I feel bad, but I am intrigued at the way it turned out and once again recognize that fishing is a tedious activity, requiring, among other factors, good timing—"bee-een dey-ah when eetz hap-neen."

Kaukau and Talk Story

An eruption and lava flow in the late 1920s forced residents to move the village a few hundred yards south. Today, the launch ramp, church, and hālau (open-air meeting house) comprise the village center near Kalani's place. Some years ago, however, a few residents were awarded a development grant to rebuild on the old settlement site. Kalani was one of these. All the new houses were built on pilings so as to allow tsunamis to pass under. Hawai'i faces the tectonically active Pacific Rim on three sides, and tidal wave events have caused damage along many island coastlines throughout the course of history. This west-facing stretch of the Big Island is no exception. The elevated garage also allows for easy storage of fishing gear and boats.

11:40 a.m. We sit at a table on the lānai (porch) on the makai side of the house. There are no screens, and the fragrant ocean breeze cools us despite the bright spring sun. Two youth beds on the porch make for open-air Polynesian-style sleeping quarters for the kids.

Kalani talks about many things, but the conversation always returns to fishing. He repeatedly mentions his appreciation for a fishing newsletter received from the state's Division of Aquatic Resources. He reports his belief that communication about ocean resource issues is crucial for the welfare of ocean resources and for the perpetuation of Native Hawaiian subsistence practices related to the sea. He also says he sometimes feels rather isolated and that the newsletter is a welcome linkage to events and activities going on in other parts of Hawai'i.

Kalani's wife, Pua (pseudonym), fixes lunch while we talk. The main course is fried ono, caught the previous day; delicious dried kāhala (*Seriola dumerili* or amberjack) with roasted garlic; and fried pāku'iku'i (*Acanthurus achilles* or achilles surgeon fish). The latter is an unusually tasty reef fish with lots of bones—a good "talk story fish." There are sides of rice and salad. Kalani's fishing friends drop by on the way to town, asking Pua if she needs anything. Clearly, a tight social network is at play here, with cooperation on many levels. The men yell up from the yard, joking that they "already forgot" which fish is Kalani's, to which he responds smartly, "Weighed 'em arr-reddie, brah, no geev me da [money for the] small wahn!" Then he yells down, "Peddle 'em in da road eef you haf to!" He then remarks to me that he hadn't planned on going to town and that he was just going to freeze the fish we caught for kaukau later on. Kalani had deemed the trip to town not worth the time, effort, and travel costs, so it is fortuitous the men are going. He expects the fish will bring $2.00 per pound.

Adding to the evidence that fish and fishing play variable, important, and spontaneous roles in local cultural and social life, soon after "da bruddahs" leave, Pua realizes that she should have taken our ono with her to the hospital where her mother, regrettably, lay ill. Many of her family are there, and she laments not having kept the fish "fo-ah to share."

The phone rings while Kalani talks about the upcoming ‘ahi season. It’s another friend asking about our trip. He retells the essence of the excursion and the current plight of the now-infamous ono. My understanding of the extent and nature of this social network and the daily importance of fish and fishing in this community is growing.

Kalani also talks about the tough times brought on by the aforementioned resort development plan. Tears come to his eyes as he tells me, “You know—no mattah whot—some of us goin’ to da end of da stream brah,” meaning that some people, including himself, feel so strongly about the long-held customs and traditions of residents that they would put their lives on the line to preserve them. He says, however, that one problem that will continue to hurt the community is the shyness and tendency toward noninvolvement that is characteristic of residents in this “country” area. The resort issue evidently brought some people together but not everyone, and Kalani fears that the community will be tested and stressed by similar issues in the future (“Dey-ah comin’ dis way”).

Kalani suggests that development of a fishing cooperative and facility might help the village fishermen and their families. He feels that formal cooperative arrangements and infrastructure would simplify icing the fish, getting them to market, and basically fishing in a more unified fashion. This leads me to wonder about the current lack of amenities here and whether the kinds of changes that a fishing co-op would bring are truly desired. I decide to ask Kalani and Pua a sensitive question and put it directly: “If you folks could get it, would you want power (electricity)?” Pua rather quickly says that she wants it *sometimes* but then defers to her husband, saying, “But I don’t think Kalani and Uncle do.” The fisherman replies pragmatically:

> You get wahn taste en want more, eh? Even da Indians in da caves have changed, yeah? . . . Dey no want go back, eh? . . . Now we have dis fancy house and eet seems like da next teeng fo-ah us to do. . . . We used to boil water fo-ah clean clothes, eh? . . . Now . . . evrie-ting changes.
>
> [You get a taste of something and you want more, yes? Even the Indians comfortable in their caves have changed and don’t want to go back to the old ways. Now we have this fancy house and getting on the grid seems the next logical thing to do. We used to have to clean our clothes by boiling them. Now, it’s getting easier. Everything changes.]

12:48 p.m. Talk story goes on and on. At one point, an elderly haole woman comes in and sits down, immediately bringing smiles to Kalani and his wife and engaging all of us in her compelling and humorous conversation about village life. She talks in local language about “so and so” and “so and so”—various village gossip.

I recognize the deep friendship of these folks and begin to feel that my mission is over for the moment; I am now becoming an obtrusive observer rather than participant. Thus, the arrival of their friend and this new conversation seems a good juncture for departure. I am near information overload anyway. So ends this part of my stay in the village. After numerous warm and protracted Polynesian good-byes, I climb into the truck and wend my way up the steep and winding path to the highway, reflecting on the other worlds that lie at the base of mighty Mauna Loa, on the northern doorstep of the South Pacific.

Analysis

Kalani clearly is an adept fisherman with great knowledge of the marine environment surrounding the village. All of his actions are practiced to the point that they appear fluid and automatic, from navigating through the treacherous reef to finding the ko'a, to gaffing and landing the fish. He is a social fisherman but also enjoys solitude at sea. He is Native Hawaiian, fully aware of his heritage and that of his village but also cognizant of the way life for his people has changed and of the further changes that are imminent. This makes him unsure and fearful of the future but also active in seeking to preserve what he sees as the best of life in the village.

Like other fishing trips I have taken in Hawai'i, this one defied easy classification. It really characterizes the flexible Hawaiian-style approach. The trip, in this case, was defined not by the motivations or desired outcomes held by Kalani but rather by the situations in which the fisherman found himself as the day progressed. He may have had some internal notion about what he might do with fish if and once they were caught, but the actual catching of the fish conditioned what kind of trip it would become and how it might be classified. In other words, it was not known beforehand precisely whether this was a trip in which the fish would be sold, kept for consumption, shared with others, or used for bait. Had no fish come up, the trip might have been classified after the fact as recreational. Indeed, after hearing through the grapevine that Kalani felt our trip was "lousy," the elderly haole woman who visited Kalani's house after lunch called it "a joyride." Viewed from the perspective of the ultimate disposition of the ono, the trip might be seen as a commercial trip because the fish was sold. But we do not know what Kalani would ultimately do with the money—whether it would be applied to pay for the fuel, in which case it might more properly be called an "expense" trip, or whether it could be counted as "profit" and, hence, a commercial trip. The situation calls for a more holistic framework of understanding.

This would apply to the concept of customary fishing as well, where *customary* and *traditional* are defined as part of a Hawaiian model with its own terms. For instance, although fishermen here *do* engage in traditional methods such as palu 'ahi, customary fishing in this case is not necessarily best defined in relation to physical methods but rather in relation to factors such as intergenerational transmission of knowledge and proper use of the marine environment, as is customary at the ancient ko'a. Local residents are currently involved in formalizing rules regarding fishing activity along the ko'a, and they are borrowing old ideas about proper management in order to do so. For instance, discussion with an elderly Hawaiian man farther north along this coastline led to his referring to an ancient text about the proper treatment of 'ōpelu. The handwritten book, held by his family for many generations, supported statements made by elderly informants elsewhere that 'ōpelu were traditionally fed with vegetable material. This was being incorporated into concepts about how to best manage resources for Kalani's village.

Native Hawaiians butchering large ʻahi "for share" on Oʻahu, late 1990s

Community is also a definable concept in this setting. Indeed, my experience here reveals a closely knit network of fishermen and assistants who are keenly aware of the movement of fish, the actions of other fishermen, local etiquette in the water, the market price of the resource, and so forth. Further, there is genuine concern and a willingness to assist other fishermen in revealing where and when the fish were caught, and in offering to take fish to the market. There is strong interdependence here. Kalani's conversation supports the idea of community, as well. For instance, he noted without my asking that cooperative efforts to fish the koʻa were what sustained villagers for many generations before and after the arrival of "outsiders."

Given the predominance of Native Hawaiian society in the area, a more appropriate model or definition of *community* might be tested. For instance, Matsuoka and colleagues (1994) suggest that the normative definition of *community* is insufficient for understanding social life in the Hawaiian village. The authors present a view in which the ʻohana, or extended family, is the central consideration in defining the term. This certainly is applicable in this village, where Kalani revealed strong feelings of kinship not only with his nuclear family but also with an extended group of friends.

In sum, I assert the power of observation in this exercise and the importance of place in relating the contemporary meanings of subsistence, custom, and community for Native Hawaiians. Subsistence in the modern context is actually a circular and opportunistic arrangement in which natural resources are components of systems of reciprocity or are sold to support subsequent harvest and consumption of additional resources. Custom tends to be functional in nature,

Alaska natives exhausted from butchering whale, near Barrow, 2001

ensuring the safety of fishermen and the availability of local resources for future use. Community is kōkua (cooperation). I could see, for instance, the close and cooperative interaction of Kalani with "da bruddahs." I can also bear witness to the deep emotions Kalani felt when he spoke of his affection for and dedication to his beloved village, for I saw the tears in his eyes.

6/Some Deeper Analysis of the Fishing Lifestyle in Hawai'i

As noted at the outset, I ultimately decided that two basic organizing principles would be useful for making sense of the mass of descriptive information compiled while working with fishermen in the Islands. The first helps address variation in the sociocultural, economic, and at-sea operational realities of the small-boat fishing endeavor in Hawai'i. The second aids in examining the nature and implications of fishing as experienced by the participants and in indicating the changes that could occur should fishing opportunities be constrained in some manner. This chapter moves toward synthesis of these concepts, summarizing key aspects of the different forms of small-boat fishing, and examining the implications of each for the fishermen involved, with emphasis placed on the nature and implications of fishing in the broader context of local and Native Hawaiian society.

THE IMPORTANCE OF HISTORY

The incentives to continue fishing despite its many challenges are quite compelling for many participants in Hawai'i's small-boat fishery. For Native Hawaiians, harvesting, sharing, and consuming fish are vital social and cultural processes. People who know the ocean and fish well are highly respected. It is important to realize that the term and concept of *kupuna* refers not only to the ancients buried in secret lava tubes or upright in the hidden sands at Ka Lae. Very significantly, it also relates to those elders who have more recently passed on and to one's living grandparents, aunties, uncles, and others who have reached an age and status of knowledge and respect. Fishing can be a venue for achieving such status.

During much of their lives, many living Native Hawaiian elders enjoyed gathering, fishing, hunting, and other aspects of a subsistence-focused lifestyle. The experiences one has interacting with such persons are often held close to the heart. They are often remembered and cherished by the keiki (children). The experiences become part of the sphere of actions and ideas contributing to one's identity as Native Hawaiian.

The importance of past experiences and their influence on life in the present cannot be overemphasized in the Hawai‘i context. But because I am an outsider reporting observations and stories communicated in the present, the importance of intergenerational communication is difficult to convey. I am reminded of a field experience wherein a kupuna talked about days past to an audience of younger Native Hawaiians. They paid rapt and respectful attention to his slowly spoken and obviously heartfelt words. The old man smoked a large cigar, periodically blowing a cloud of blue smoke up toward to the ceiling and the shadows of the room, where it lingered, shot through in places with beams of sunlight that early Hawaiian morning. He spoke joyfully of days long gone, of fishing with his makua kāne and uncles and of playing in the mountains with his siblings. Hukilau (fishing with nets, community-style) was common. Life was difficult at times, but he was strong and free. Then his face hardened as he spoke of being punished in school for speaking Hawaiian and, later, of being held for treason just after establishment of statehood. He had tried to organize resistance to the destruction of ancient gravesites surrounding his little village prior to development of a large resort, and he was held in jail for some time.

The wonders and injustices of the past are not lost on Native Hawaiian youth today. Moreover, given the difficulties of plantation life among immigrants and the challenges of more recent economic conditions in Hawai‘i, remembrance of challenging times and situations is common among many local residents. Many dislike and resist the people and ideologies that have made it so. As one of my informants told me:

> Free-keeng how-lee guys. Always moveen so fast. Always try kaht ’em down, build ’em ahp. No can be laid back—Why-in-style. Just mellow, eh? We hated howlees grow-een ahp, you know. Hated ’em. Locals hate haoles, did you know that?

This is a generalized assessment to be sure but is clearly indicative of problems brought by haoles over the course of time. Now, daily life involves rent and mortgage payments, car and truck payments, education costs, the IRS, pressures to perform in a certain way, and so on.

On one hand, people are constrained or enabled by historical processes. People inherit or do not inherit wealth from their forebears and often are influenced by ideas and knowledge from previous generations. On the other hand, people generate new enabling and constraining conditions for themselves in contemporary society. In order to understand how social and economic conditions perpetuate over time, these hands have to be seen as joined.

Native Hawaiians, whose ancestors were divested of land and often forced to assimilate a way of life quite different from their own, now often operate with little material inheritance and engage cultural norms and values that are rooted more deeply in cooperation and reciprocity than in capitalism. I refer especially to norms and values developed during periods of Hawaiian history when cooperation was so vital to survival, as was the case, for instance, following the Great Mahele in the mid-nineteenth century. Then, a new economic order was being imposed that for most led to a subsistence-oriented way of life wherein a little cash was stretched a long way and natural resources were used extensively. Fish from loko i‘a (fish ponds), fish from the open sea, reef fish, shellfish, and limu

The joys of fishing start early in Hawai'i

were among the most important foods. Kōkua and mālama (stewardship) of resources were critical in making this adaptive system work.

Adhering to such norms and values enabled survival for many families, and subsistence-oriented lifestyles and sharing of resources in the 'ohana setting continue to be critically important among many Hawaiians to this day. For the fishermen who participated in this study, fishing often is a continuation of something they took to early in life in this context. Youth today often help with the fishing operations. It is sometimes the case that when young men get involved in fishing early on, they will latch on to it and get involved as crew members, learn how to harvest food for the 'ohana and earn a little cash, and perhaps eventually buy or inherit a boat for themselves. Thus, the activity enables many Native Hawaiians and local persons to participate in a form of work that is a platform for perpetuating dearly held traditions and social interaction in the 'ohana and community settings. It can also reduce feelings of alienation and other problems inherent in the "normal" workplace and is a good alternative to some of the temptations of the street. On the other hand, when youth engage in fishing in an avid way, in a way that pulls them away from school, for instance, it can limit options later in life, at least within the economic system predominant in the Islands today. Fishing can be a difficult way to earn a living, let alone get ahead. Such is the unforgiving nature of competitive capitalist society, and the conundrum currently faced by many in the Islands.

REAL RELIEF

For many who do end up pursuing jobs in the mainstream world of work, fishing can provide a means of escape from stress and pressure. This was commonly mentioned by Island fishermen as a primary reason for fishing. Generally speaking, Americans are known for working hard, though people often work toward

Relaxation and social interaction by radio, offshore O'ahu, 1997

materialistic goals that ultimately do not satisfy even if they can manage to meet them. Fishing is said to offer such satisfaction, and fishermen with land-based jobs sometimes forego hours at work for the happiness and relaxation fishing brings them. A readily offered perspective among many fishermen is that "life is for living." There also is a common sense that death will come soon enough and that missing the joys of life in Hawai'i, such as fishing, is foolishness.

I have met quite a few war veterans while working in Hawai'i. Some report finding a sense of peace and freedom on the water, an escape from haunting memories. For some, the ocean is a pacific force. Being on the ocean, interacting with like-minded fishermen, developing one's own skills, and providing food for the 'ohana are fishing-specific factors that can assist in recovery from the terrors of war.

FISHING AND LOCAL CULTURE

Fishing is an inherently social activity. It is within the context of the small group that so many fishermen appear to find achievement and satisfaction.

I have thus far described a system of cooperation, etiquette, norms, and ideologies that are part and parcel of how fishing works in Hawai'i. People behave in a certain way to effect a culture of fishing. Part of what defines that culture is the way people who engage in it distinguish themselves from the rest of society. For instance, people who don't know and have never experienced Hawai'i are seen by locals as malihini or "fresh off da plane." In this maritime setting, accomplished fishermen are the antithesis of that. The process of distinguishing between the two operates even within this small society and helps the participants define it and their place therein. The "weekend warrior" is way down on the hierarchy of achieved status, and the hard-core troller or revered kupuna is at the top.

In a more general sense, local and Native Hawaiian people often differentiate between themselves and other groups. Analysis of modern culture in Hawaii would be lacking without some discussion of this phenomenon. The tendency is common, and given the course of history, it is quite understandable. Differentiating from haoles can be a form of resistance to certain ideologies and behaviors that are in the mainstream on the Continent and that leak over into the Islands. As a result, it is often hard for a haole, even one who has lived in Hawai'i for decades, to be wholeheartedly accepted by a tight-knit group of Native Hawaiian fishermen, though I have witnessed an equal amount of aloha and acceptance, at least on the surface.

But acceptance isn't necessarily co-identification. People in Hawai'i do commonly discuss others' backgrounds—that is, who is from which family, where so and so came from, the nature of one's ethnic heritage. There is differentiation between ethnicities all around but more accommodation within *local* society than between *locals* and haoles. Even hapa (ethnically mixed) individuals whose background includes Caucasian ancestry but who meet the other requirements are considered fully *local.*

The core of this business of ethnic relations and identification in Hawai'i relates directly to the social process of being and being recognized as Native Hawaiian and/or *local*. This is a complex and sensitive topic in Hawai'i. Field-oriented anthropologists specialize in their ability to develop working relationships with persons in strange settings, in places where cultural patterns are unfamiliar. Hawai'i is unique in this regard in that so many people and cultural

Social Scene at O'ahu Harbor, 1999

patterns are operating concurrently in a bounded island setting. The situation is so complex, in fact, that an overarching social system has developed. People maintain customs and other cultural attributes unique to their ethnic heritage(s) but now also share aspects of a more generalized pattern of culture called *local.*

Long-term local residence is an important requisite for participating in *local* society, but there's more to it. For instance, a haole can live in Hawai'i for decades and gain acceptance among non-haole *locals* as kama'āina, but this achieved status may not be recognized even in the adjacent valley. It certainly does occur, but a haole widely accepted as *local* today is relatively rare and appears to require both lifelong or very long-term residence and locally appropriate behavior. I recall a Caucasian political candidate, who was born and lived his entire life on O'ahu, being told in a public setting to "go home, haole boy" because one of his stated perspectives was dissimilar to that of an important local constituency. Moreover, although being a haole whose forebears were born in Hawai'i generations ago confers inherited kama'āina status, this is not necessarily endearing because such a person may be associated with missionaries or plantation owners who are perceived by some to have wreaked much havoc in the Islands. Being a person "of color," as the term is used on the Continent, doesn't define *local* status either and, generally speaking, pōpolos (persons of African ancestry) are in the same situation as haoles for achieving *local* status.

Perhaps the most basic requirement for being readily identified as *local* is a genetic heritage that enables one to be visually recognized by other *locals* as being part or pure Native Hawaiian or Pacific Islander, or belonging to one or more of the non-Caucasian genetic groups present in Hawai'i during the Plantation era or soon thereafter: Japanese, Chinese, Portuguese, Filipino, Puerto Rican, and Korean. But it must be said, too, that as the original residents of Hawai'i, some kanaka maoli (indigenous Hawaiians) see themselves as distinct and to be distinguished from other groups that comprise relatively recently developed *local* society.

Tenure of residence and visual characteristics are central to being recognized as *local.* But in actuality, things are yet a bit more complex. There are cultural and behavioral requirements as well. A *local* person looks, talks, acts, and dresses in ways best attained by exposure from birth ("born and raised") or through long-term assimilative practice. Thus, although a person from Japan or Tonga may arrive in the Islands possessing the necessary genetic features for being recognized as *local,* he or she wouldn't fit the bill until speech, mannerisms, and dress were clearly *local* in nature. In this regard, although haoles may not *look local,* it is possible for them to acquire the necessary behavioral characteristics and so enhance the possibility of acceptance (or again, in some instances, maintain full *local* status). Further, haoles and locals alike may be labeled as more or less *haole* (and by extension, more or less *local*).

I don't mean to indicate that people cannot or do not in the end peacefully coexist in Hawai'i. Indeed, deep friendships and lasting marriages can be and are forged across all of these "lines" of ethnicity. Rather, I seek to understand and communicate what to me is an interesting and often subtle process of sociocultural differentiation and to make sense of certain social interactions I have witnessed in the Islands, some of which indicate underlying tension.

An experience in a village on the Big Island provides a useful example in which lifelong residents (in this case Native Hawaiian fishermen) and haole visitors interact in perfunctory fashion but ultimately remain segregated. The haoles dressed in local fashion and shook hands local style. The residents were friendly enough. But there was something missing:

> Directly north of the *hālau,* about 60 yards away, three middle-aged Native Hawaiian fishermen and their sons were sitting and milling about in the backyard of a house adjacent to a small promontory along the shore. The older men revealed large, unclothed bellies and extensive tattoos. One intricate tattoo resembled a thick lei around one man's neck. The teens were also tattooed but very muscular. The group was preparing for a lū'au. A pickup pulled up to drop off beer and other party supplies. A fire was started, and a makeshift rotisserie (for huli-huli) was put together for the roasting of a small boar. The boar was skewered from 'ōkole to mouth (nuku) and basted with a short bamboo pole wrapped with part of a towel soaked in some unknown liquid. The fire was tended with a bamboo pole about 6 feet in length. There was little wind; thus, the smoke rose generally straight up. As time passed, more people showed up, including a group of three heavyset, bearded *haoles,* dressed in T-shirts and rubber slippers. Ukuleles were played beautifully by the Hawaiians. The haoles shook hands with the Hawaiians and spoke with them briefly. But members of each group were soon talking and drinking among themselves. The haoles stayed for an hour or so, expressed their thanks, and departed. The pā'ina (celebration) lasted well into the night. (Field notes, 1998)

Everybody's ethnic and genetic differences matter at some level in Hawai'i. I am not talking about discrimination or prejudice, although these certainly exist here, as everywhere. Rather, the very act of recognizing and discussing differences is part of *local* culture itself ("dat guy so haole," "her auntie Portagee," "dey so pah-kay," "Uncle pure Why-in," and so forth) There can be tension, to be sure, but humor as well, and the system seems to work somehow. In short, an established social order has developed and is continually tendered in this context of unparalleled diversity.

For Native Hawaiians, group identification and differentiation from others is staying the erosion of a culture with roots in deep antiquity. One marker involves use of the Hawaiian language. Although fluent speakers of Hawaiian are more common in some areas than others, language programs and advocates of cultural renaissance encourage its use, and many youth are now speaking this mellifluous language.

At a more general level, the ability to speak what was once called Hawaiian Creole English, now evolved into a modern version called "pidgin," is an important marker of *local* status. Besides being hard for the outsider to understand, an inability to speak it well makes it abundantly clear that the speaker is from elsewhere, with immediate loss of status inasmuch as status is ascribed to persons who have grown up here or have been here a long time. In her book *My Time in Hawai'i,* Victoria Nelson (1989:41–47) offers much insight into the phenomenon of *local* in Hawai'i and the concomitant importance of speaking pidgin as a first language. She describes this form of speech as "earthy, funny, succinct, never inarticulate [and] above all an expression of solidarity against the incursion of haoles in the broadest sense of the term, that is, the non-Island born of all races." The language is indeed succinct and articulate—speakers convey much meaning through few words, as notable in the previous passages of local "talk story."

Unfortunately, always speaking pidgin can serve to limit opportunities in a larger American society of ethnocentric actors who cannot or do not appreciate its qualities. Yet, many *locals* can use pidgin or regular English interchangeably, depending on context. In fact, in a more general sense, *locals* move easily between mainstream American *and* local cultural settings, and additionally within those of their own ethnic heritage(s). Some possess the ability and skills to both identify themselves with and differentiate themselves from multiple ethnic groups in Hawai'i. In sum, *locals* are Americans who are akamai (highly knowledgeable) of multiple cultures, including the overarching culture of *local.* The typical haole arriving in Hawaii is not so well versed and has much to learn (including the local importance of fish and fishing). The haole tourist in this setting is a mere passerby.

INTER-FLEET DIFFERENTIATION

Individual fishermen I've worked with tend to identify with the larger group of "small-boat fishermen." Arguably, this group has distinct interests, needs, and concerns relative to other fishing fleets in the region. For instance, many small-boat operators blame longline fishing operations for what they see as declining pelagic fish resources. Further, there is directed accusation against "foreign" vessels in this regard, a term that many fishermen in the late 1990s used to refer to captains of Vietnamese ancestry.

Such persons have a less extensive history of presence in Hawai'i than do others whose forbears hailed from other Asian nations. Local Koreans, for instance, have a relatively longer tenure and reportedly enjoy more extensive integration, hence greater acceptance from the larger community of fishermen in Hawai'i. At about the time I was fishing with captains in Hawai'i, fishermen of Vietnamese ancestry were having a hard time of it. Members of this group appeared to be going through initial stages of assimilating into *local* culture. One of my informants, a Native Hawaiian troll fisherman from O'ahu, revealed his thoughts about fishermen of Vietnamese ancestry who had been using gill nets inside the 40-fathom ledge in a manner long considered kapu by locals—dragging the bottom and thereby damaging coral:

> Feesh num-bah wahn in [this town]. If you can speak da language [the language of local fishing] den you okay. But if no can . . . . Dey cannot. . . . Dey got kicked out of da Gulf . . . but dey gettin' loans he-ah ennyway and no pay taxes . . . and dey *can* speak English, brah, just say dey cannot. . . . Dey flooding da market, make it tahf fo-ah da small kine guy. . . . Hey, eet wahn keek in da pants brah.
>
> [Fish and fishing are number one in this town. If you can speak the language of our local style of fishing, then you will be okay. But if you can't, . . . They cannot. They got kicked out of the Gulf [in truth, much of the fleet in question has been highly productive and adaptive in that region]. But they are getting loans here anyway and they

don't pay taxes [speculative]. And they *can* speak English, my friend. They just say they cannot. They are flooding the market and making it tough for the small-boat operator. Hey, it's really a kick in the pants.]

Identity as fishermen develops and plays out in various ways and places. In this case, representatives of the various small-boat cohorts essentially say, "We are fishermen, we are Hawaiian fishermen, we are local fishermen, we are good fishermen, we are doing it right, we are different from the others," and so forth. These assessments are indeed correct in many cases, and the process of differentiation serves to elevate the status of group membership while furthering the requirements for being a member. Succeeding in meeting these qualifications, belonging to this or that exclusive group, and achieving status within that group further explains why people here carry forward with the small-boat fishing lifestyle.

Yet, such distinctions can be superseded by challenges imposed from without, such as those that appear imminent given internationally determined allocation of migratory fish resources in the Pacific. Further, fishing is challenging for virtually all operators, and captains and owners of even the largest fishing vessels in Hawai'i struggle with market-related factors and resource challenges. Insofar as distinctions limit cooperation that might be advantageous to Island fishermen in general, participants in any given fleet may consider coalescing to ensure survival.

VALUING SKILL AND CUSTOMS

Modern small-boat fishermen in Hawai'i are variably knowledgeable of fishing and the ocean environment. Long years of involvement and exposure to knowledgeable mentors lead to personal knowledge and skill. The accomplished reveal an intimate knowledge of the ocean environment, the weather, the moon, swells, and sea states. Such persons know the habits of pelagic species, the smaller fish on which they feed, and the birds that accompany these. They know where and when to go to find fish and how to get there. They know the best manner of pursuit, and they possess and use a code of ethics about fishing and the proper size of fish to take. They know what gear to use, when to use it, and why. Such knowledge is often initially transmitted to youth through the words of the elders who, in turn, were schooled by their kupuna. Application of such knowledge, coupled with trial and error, characterizes the process of learning.

The basic material aspects of trolling remain fairly constant. An important exception is the rapid development of communications and positioning technologies. These have significantly increased the efficiency of the small-boat fleet and the potential for social interaction on the water.

Learning how to fish well and in keeping with local expectations is a social process. Beginners are schooled in various ways. Mistakes can lead to chastisement, especially when these compromise the safety of others or the ability of others to catch fish. Viewed in total, this process leads to and perpetuates working systems of navigation and fishing. The strength and scope of those systems vary depending on the setting. Along the more rural stretches of the coastline of Hawai'i, for instance, locally enforced patterns of etiquette and custom have

Scene at customary funeral for a fisherman, O'ahu

developed. These exist on O'ahu as well, although the greater number of vessels operating on that island makes for a more dynamic situation in which newcomers and locals are more likely to interact, at times with some initial conflict. I am reminded of a near fatal occurrence in 1998 in which a haole man on a jet ski became entangled in the lines of a local troll fisherman. The event did not advance the status of the general category of haole newcomers in the eyes of many in the local fleet.

MALES, FEMALES, AND FISHING: IN HAWAI'I

The relative absence of females directly participating in the Hawai'i small-boat fishery is of great interest to me. Females are largely absent in most places where I've studied cultural aspects of fishing, but it's strikingly so here in Hawai'i. Women *do* participate indirectly: transporting fish to the auction, purchasing ice, doing palapala (paper work), and so forth. Survey work indicated that captain's wives undertook 60 percent of secondary participation, and captain's mothers and daughters undertook another 12 percent. Relatively extensive indirect involvement of women in small-boat fishing in Hawai'i articulates with similar findings in dissimilar settings (see, for example, Davis and Nadel-Klein 1988, and Thiessen et al. 1992). But I argue that the Hawai'i situation is more profound and bound up with local history and social process than it is elsewhere.

Sometimes men hearken back to ancient kapus in the modern context to differentiate male roles from female roles. Other fishermen claim that women get seasick easily and so are not suited to fishing. My data suggest that, for whatever reason, women generally have not had the same opportunities to participate in

Boats, trucks, trailers, outriggers, gear: O'ahu 1999

boat fishing as have men. In this case, what may be at work is role differentiation and an associated lack of opportunity for women to gain their sea legs, to grow accustomed to Hawaiian swell and sea conditions. For men who have grown up fishing, few days present conditions to which they have not become accustomed. This is not to say that men do not experience discomfort in rough seas. Indeed, rough conditions invariably lead even the most experienced to utter muted comments, such as "tough on my back," "damn rough out there today," "beat us to death," or, in local vernacular, "get dirty lickins." But women generally do not grow up boat fishing in the Islands, or even if they do, they tend to move on to other roles as they grow older. It may also be the case that tendency toward discomfort is equally distributed across both sexes but that unaffected males gravitate toward fishing whereas, in the case of Hawai'i, potentially unaffected women often are not encouraged or given the opportunity. Persons of both sexes who experience seasickness obviously tend to stay ashore.

In any event, for the majority of local operators to include women directly and regularly in the fishing enterprise would undoubtedly disrupt the way the fishery has been organized over the years. By including women directly on board or in making decisions about it vis-à-vis the household, the enterprise could be threatened, in part because it is not always a profitable venture.

Women sometimes confront the men on this, and many fishermen report that fishing is a source of contention in the household. I asked the widow of an avid fisherman what she thought about men fishing. Here is some of her telling dialogue:

> It's okay if they're serious about it and make a good living at it. I think it's age-related. When guys are younger, they're more rebellious. They think they can do anything. Guys are so egocentric! But when they get married, they realize they have to start making money. But he was always telling me, "Well, the moon wasn't right,"

Hula dancer performing at O'ahu fishing tournament

> or, "The fish weren't there," or something. It gets to be too much sometimes. But it's what guys do, I guess. They see it as a manly kind of thing. If it's providing food for the table, that's one thing, but when it's just going out to be with the guys and [excessive] drinking and all that, I don't know. If it's neglecting the family and he's never around. . . . And if you gotta have a boat then, you know, you have to have a way to pay for it, and it was taking away from the family. It was alright when we were younger, but. . . . [Did he ever take you out with him?] Yeah, once or twice. But I remember [laughs], they took me out one time and gave me the lures with the tails bitten off. . . . I kept wondering what they were laughing at!

THE IMPORTANCE OF PEAK EXPERIENCE

There is yet another viable explanation for why fishermen tend to do what they do, whether it's commercial, recreational, or customary in nature. As physical beings whose life experiences always register in the memory, we are all influenced by our past. Researchers are beginning to delve deep within the brain, uncovering a vast and intricate system of neurons, neurotransmitters, enzymatic responses, hormonal feedback loops, and so forth. Good and bad experiences alike make an impression in our psyche via such physiological pathways. Clearly, there is a behavioral tendency to reproduce the positive impressions and avoid the negative.

Fishing in Hawai'i can provide unforgettably positive experiences, and people continually seek these. Experiences in the field and conversations with fishermen make clear that the peak experiences achieved while fishing are central to continuation of the activity. Playing and working with others to achieve hana pa'a are part of "talk story" for days, weeks, and years to come. Even among a captain's collection of fishing experiences, one or two always stand out and bear retelling. These can be amazing tales in the Hawai'i context of small boats, giant swells, and potentially huge fish!

Such peak experiences register in people's brains, and they often seek to relive them in discussion with others and in similar real-time situations. Although peak experiences can certainly occur in solo, sharing or reliving the experience with others adds a dimension Native Hawaiians might term *lōkahi* (unity). Thus, it is useful to consider the physicality of experience as registered in the brain as one explanation for why people revisit fishing and the social experiences it involves. Much adrenaline can be involved in hooking a big fish and dealing with giant swells, with a release of endorphins at the end of the day! Although we can never fully recreate the social element of experience, the memory and its biophysical correlates may be enough to inspire us to try. People *have* passed on, or they are doing other things. There will never be an afternoon just like the one with Uncle Kawika in the mid-70s when "we caught da kine giant a'u Hilo side." But the experience created a deeply ingrained memory and experiential knowledge that fishing can bring great joy. For many, there is ongoing interest in replicating that kind of experience, and providing it for others.

Summary notes from work in a particularly remote area of the Big Island provide some indication of the rich social context in which fishing is played out in Hawai'i. Of note, the fishery associated with the context described here has diminished significantly since the fieldwork was undertaken in the late 1990s, largely due to economic constraints and changes in local marketing opportunities. The experience is memorable in many ways—for the observer, for the informant who did not want to forget, and for the background actors whose lives revolved around the setting and activity of summer ika-shibi fishing along the black lava coast of Hawai'i Island:

> The late summer sun sinks slowly toward the horizon, coloring the towering tropical clouds with subtle shades of orange and pink. It is prime fishing season here, and a procession of small boats leaves the access ramp to fish overnight. Most fishermen seek to make some cash, though some fish will be cut into poke, grilled, or otherwise consumed upon their return. Captain after captain backs his truck down the steep ramp to release boat from trailer. Mates rush to moor vessels at the small dock while drivers park the rusty trucks. Then it's off through the harbor entrance to secret fishing spots far from shore for a night of setting bait, pulling lines, and balancing bodies against seas and swells. Community is observable here, and there is great beauty in the rugged surroundings. Local families cook meat and fish on grills and open fires along the black sand beach, under the canopy of tall palms and flowering plants. Aunties and uncles sit quietly, talking in soft tones as they watch the fleet depart and the exploits of the older kids and young adults who surf and swim just offshore.
>
> Given its depth, the ramp area doubles as a swimming pool for keiki not old enough to play in the larger swells beyond the jetty. The area is treacherous for navigation, with kids swimming near outboard engines and the lurching swells threatening to crush boats against the short seawall. The harbor entrance is narrow and large swells sometimes span its width, forcing captains to wait attentively until the wave trains pass or, if need be, to rush forward up the steep faces and then quickly throttle down, letting the wave pass under without smashing vessel in the trough behind.

Summer memories in the making, Pohoiki, Hawai'i Island, late 1990s

The smell of outboard motor oil and fish is thick in the air. I listen to the sounds: the crashing surf, the whine of engines, and the gleeful sounds of kids swimming, wrestling, and jumping about along the shoreline. Walking along the high lava-rock seawall, I eventually gain a good vantage point on the action. A small steel-framed lighthouse is emplaced at the terminal end of the jetty. At its feet sits a large basket made of ti leaves (*Cordyline fruticosa*) filled with orchids and ginger flowers—an offering.

I notice a fisherman backing his vessel down the ramp with no mate to assist. Once the boat is freed of its trailer, however, a young wahine (Hawaiian woman) rushes forward to quickly grab the bowline while standing on the dock. She holds the boat steady despite surging swells and current as the fisherman parks his truck. Once boarded, he takes the line from her hand and prepares to depart while she climbs the few steps up to the seawall and turns to face the ocean. I move toward her, sensing she will tell me something about fishing from this little refuge. But then I notice tears in her eyes. She sees me watching the tears roll down her cheeks and speaks softly without my asking: "My husband lost at sea lass week; hees partner go-eeng out for da first time wit-out him." We stand together for some moments before I back away into my own thoughts, wanting to help but knowing I cannot.

EXTERNAL FORCES

Economic factors are particularly challenging to small-boat fishermen in Hawai'i. Commercial fishing often doesn't really pay off; holoholo fishing can

In memoriam

pay enough to cover some expenses, and although subsistence fishing provides food and satisfaction and perhaps cash to go again tomorrow, it generally does not pay the bills. People who fish commercially on a full- or part-time basis and people who fish for consumptive and customary purposes are particularly vulnerable to the challenges of the predominant economic system in Hawai'i. In the case of commercial fishing, returns on investment often are scant in large part due to conditions at the marketplace. These conditions, in turn, relate to other factors, not the least of which is public recognition of and willingness to pay full value for the labor involved in harvesting seafood. For subsistence-oriented fishermen, a traditional lifestyle limits one's ability to accrue capital that might aid in meeting the many demands of life in modern society. But in both cases, the participants focus on fishing in part because life in the mainstream world of work is often unsatisfying or not pertinent to one's real goals in life. As one informant asserted on numerous occasions: "Not everie-body like be wahn law-yah o-ah wahn dahk-tah brah!" ["Not everyone wants to be a lawyer or a doctor!"]

This suggests that the fishermen are aware of limitations inherent in the fishing way of life. But it seems, too, that one can walk down a path for a while before directly experiencing its dangers. In the case of fishing, the longer-term risks are not necessarily seen very clearly because of necessarily overt attention to the short term. Indeed, I have observed that commercial fishermen and persons who hunt, fish, and gather, and supplement those activities with different kinds of part-time wage work or other forms of income tend to be focused on the moment—in terms of avoiding immediate physical risks, making ends meet on a daily basis, and enjoying the moments at sea in a culturally appropriate manner. The focus is on the now: following the bite, working the tide carefully, interacting with others to succeed *this week, today*. In fact, fishing *demands* attention in the moment. Being there at the right tide, at the right moment, is often critical for success, with some luck thrown in, too. But success in fishing is never

Reef fish landed on the wa'a pā, Big Island, late 1990s

guaranteed, and a backup plan is useful. Thus, when Bruddah Tom calls with a little side job when the fish aren't biting ("Hey brah, can help wit da drywall?" or "Hey, get one beeg ex-cah-vay-shun brah—like work?"), the fisherman thinks about it, works out a plan, and perhaps decides the cash will come in handy. Perhaps it will cover the next fishing trip or a new carburetor for the boat ("Eh, Tahh-mee—yeah, like try work em' out brah . . . We go.").

This is economic rationality in the short term. Of course, fishermen do also have some vision of the future. But for all the reasons discussed in the previous chapters—enjoyment of the ocean, honing of skills, social norms, self-identity, group membership, attention to history and to community, and blatant rejection of the ways of the haole—the nonrecreational fisherman remains active in an oft-beloved way of life. Sometimes participants talk "junk" about fishing and about getting out of it. But the lifestyle seems to stick with them, and even if they leave for a time, they tend to come back. Some succeed in juggling part-time fishing with wage-based work and keep fishing at a level that does not detract significantly from the household income. Others are avid and prioritize fishing above all else, with various consequences. Yet others seem to succeed to varying degrees in a subsistence-oriented way of life, enabled by kōkua. But in the latter two cases, the fishermen and their families often tend to be in tedious economic situations. While analysis of history reveals the effects of changes arriving from elsewhere, it is not abundantly clear that the fishermen and others are prepared to deal with the globalizing forces now bearing down on the Hawaiian Islands.

CAPITALISM AND CHANGE IN HAWAI'I

Meanwhile—in Tokyo, Los Angeles, Honolulu—men and women in sharp business suits transact capital that is absolutely out of scale with the average fisherman's view of the local world. That capital is enjoined by a host of developers who seek opportunities in Hawai'i and by persons who seek to build, to develop, to "grow Hawai'i's economy." Although the Japanese and U.S. recessions of the late 1990s diminished the rate of development in Hawai'i, such situations are cyclic in nature. Not long into the new century, in fact, numerous reports of new development plans around the island were announced, and real estate is at a premium once again.

Many of the fishermen who participated in this study are part-time construction workers. Thus, although resorts and new homes may provide job opportunities for members of the small-boat fleet, the scale of benefits must be considered. The scales of difference in investment and profit are incredibly different, and the monies earned by fishermen are but a drop in an ocean of globalizing capital arriving on these shores at the start of the twenty-first century. The apparent benefits are actually masked liabilities because such development will serve to escalate local land values and tax rates. People who rent will be displaced, and, in some cases, eminent domain will displace homeowners. Beach access increasingly will be limited, and a tendency toward privatized moorings and the associated increase in costs seem likely. Boat traffic and pressure on the resources will increase. I don't need to cite any literature here or provide an academic explanation. I have personally experienced radical population growth in the coastal zone and its many consequences, including closure of much-loved fisheries. Coastal areas of the United States are now extremely valuable and desirable, and there presently is no clear policy or other distinct mechanism for preserving small societies and place-based lifestyles. Native Hawaiian land rights activists are intimately and sadly aware of this fact.

Kalani and other subsistence-oriented fishermen see this. They see more change coming. Kalani and the residents of Ka Lae described at the outset of this case study envision resistance as one answer. Some also perceive a need to get their children through school so the 'ohana and its members might achieve some measure of upward mobility or political power. They increasingly recognize a need to "beat 'them' at their own game."

But for many fishermen in Hawai'i, there is so much to be enjoyed in fishing. There is too much history and tradition to attend to. There is too much about being in Hawai'i in the here and now to abandon in favor of the *possibility* of an advance that would require so much time, effort, and uncertain return. Many Native Hawaiians and other local residents opt for a life on the ocean rather than worrying and working for years to advance in a historically oppressive system, one that, in the end, may deny real opportunity and satisfaction anyway. Some Native Hawaiians perceive a need to "go mainland" for opportunity. But this often is a distasteful prospect because of the presence of one's 'ohana in Hawai'i, deep-rootedness in the Islands, and perceptions and real stories about challenges elsewhere.

Again, there is some generalization in this assessment. Many Native Hawaiians and locals are doing well in economic terms in Hawai'i and elsewhere. The point I am attempting to make here is that the combined effects of historical factors and culturally meaningful ways of living in the present that tend to incorporate traditional values—illustrated here through the case of small-boat fishing—can serve to attenuate the likelihood of a broadly conceived population to successfully resist the agents and forces of the predominant capitalist system.

By structuring lives around fishing, participants cannot readily accumulate the capital or the power to truly resist the changes that threaten their way of life. Commercial fishermen struggle with risk, long workdays, and cyclic return on investment. There is little time for anything else in a given week. Subsistence- and custom-oriented fishing enable acquisition of food and practice of traditions, but these are threatened by forces only temporarily forestalled by grassroots opposition. People who fish on a recreational basis typically seek relaxation and a way to get on the ocean and continue various traditions. In this case, successfully transcending class position and attaining positions of power in the larger society could take so much time and effort that it might limit one's time and investment in the enjoyable and relaxing act of fishing.

Perhaps more than anywhere else in the United States, people in Hawai'i, or rather *local* and Native Hawaiian people living in Hawai'i, are aware of ethnic, cultural, and class nuances. Native Hawaiians are well aware of what are often seen as the trappings of the haole world. But some such persons are also very deeply involved in ways of life, like fishing, that will not readily be abandoned so that limited time and resources might be applied to holding off the deleterious effects of the incursions of that world.

The following notes from a day of fishing along a stretch of beach on the Big Island provide some indication of what is desirable to the participants about fishing Hawaiian-style. Jobs and money and ladders to success are meaningless in this culturally meaningful moment in time. I follow these notes, for the sake of contrast and illustration of highly dissimilar value systems, with reflexive summary notes from recent interactions with enterprising haole realty agents on O'ahu. These settings and their respective actors are quite distinct in many ways, and their attributes seem to extend history into the present. The Hawaiians continue an old way of life that emphasizes the importance of cooperation and knowing the natural world. The haoles seek to further their individual economic well-being by transferring title to pieces of the 'āina. Inevitably, these value systems will continue to clash, with ever uncertain implications for the future of Hawai'i and the descendants of its original residents.

With Native Hawaiian fishermen on the beach, Hawai'i Island:

Michael Ho'omanalo (a pseudonym but a common mix of English and Hawaiian names that is illustrative of coexisting cultural systems) agrees to take me fishing in the wa'a pā or three-board canoe. We prepare to leave from the beach along a cove fronting a little village on the Big Island. Five men and four boys assemble at the beach and confer quietly, elbows resting on the back of Terry's pickup.

Michael lays out the plan for this sunny day. He speaks with authority like a chief, and all are silent until he finishes his sentences. At his command, all nine help get the canoe past the surf zone. But only four remain in the canoe to go fishing. The rest drive or walk off to work or play, having stated they will return later in the day to assist in bringing the boat back to the beach. Terry is going back up to his mauka homestead to tend to pigs and cattle. But Michael assures him he will get a share of the catch later in the day. There is exchange of goods and close social relations between residents of sea and mountain portions of this valley, as in old Hawai'i.

Preparing to fish: Village scene on rural Hawai'i Island, 1999

We troll for ono over the ko'a with basic rods, reels, and plastic lures. We are on our way out to a secret dive spot. Upon arrival, I'm told to stay in the canoe to keep it in one spot with a handmade wooden paddle. This part of the coast is very remote, and the fishermen tell me about rich 'opihi grounds nearby. They decry what they consider poaching by strangers in this, their area of kuleana (responsibility). Their calm voices rise and demeanors harden as they relate the situation. The men dive with Hawaiian slings, regularly surfacing for breath but diving quickly back under. I note the intricate rope lashing that holds 'iako (booms) to the canoe. The craft is primitive relative to the 40-foot charter vessels out on the horizon. But it is highly functional in this setting. The small outboard powers the boat sufficiently so as to attain trolling speed but burns little fuel and can be tilted upward in the shallows. The boat draws very little water and the ama (pontoon) keeps it stable in the rolling swell. The men are visibly elated as they hoist their stringers of reef fish over the gunwales.

The trolling is unproductive on the trip home, but when we arrive at the beach later in the day, the reef fish are divided among the original nine participants. There are many smiles and handshakes, and community is observable. Terry has returned with some kalo (*Colocasia esculenta* or taro) to share with Michael and his 'ohana.

With haole realtors on the beach, O'ahu:

I am attempting to interact with realtors on behalf of a friend on the Continent who has a fair amount of capital available for investment. A bejeweled young woman picks me up in a fancy new car, pointing out various properties along the way. I know that once these lots are developed it will be that much harder for locals to access the ocean.

We meet the owner–realtor at the beachfront lot. The views are spectacular, and the ocean is steps away. The quarter-acre is listed at $1.2 million.

Multimillion dollar lots and limited access on the north shore of O'ahu

Partway through describing the property and its boundaries, the owner makes a call to his partner. Returning, he says that because much of the preliminary paperwork has been completed, he and his partner are going to ask for more than $1.2 million, perhaps as much as $1.6 million. "Oh," I think to myself, stunned not only at the $400,000 price hike but also at the whole deal—the oceanfront lot on O'ahu, the views of mountain and ocean, the white sand beach, all quite beyond my comprehension as someone who grew up constantly longing for a mere glimpse of that wide expanse of salt water. Can such relatively eternal things truly be owned by human beings whose lives here are invariably limited to a few moments in time?

Assuming my friend has significant cash in hand for a down payment, the female realtor asks the male realtor on my behalf whether cash would "sweeten the deal." "Well, no, not really," the man says with what I can only describe as muted pomposity, "I have all the cash I need." He then proceeds to describe his holdings—"five million dollars in cash" here, "two-point-five million in equity" there, "eight-hundred-fifty thousand in this project," "a half million in that project," "two homes here," "three homes on the mainland," and so on. I don't really know what to say, except a half-baked, "Wow." I suspect my lack of real interest shows through. I can't take my eyes off the ocean, sparkling as it is in the late winter sun, huge surf breaking along the distant reef.

7/Conclusions

It is difficult to predict a fully contented future here for Hawaiian fishermen. Perhaps that is because in Hawai'i the future is so deeply tied to the past. One reality of the past is that of an indigenous population overrun by people who were imperialistic in their quest to control the Islands and the economic and strategic potential of the region. The results were devastating for Native Hawaiians. The immigrant populations that have arrived and stayed in Hawai'i have also encountered various challenges.

Hawai'i has long been of great strategic interest to people in foreign governments. From the perspective of kanaka maoli, the United States is one of those nations, and many people do not recognize state or federal title to or jurisdiction over land and sea in Hawai'i. But even as some Hawaiians denounce the history of federal acquisition of Hawai'i as imperialist, the political economy as imposed, and typical American cultural ideologies as hegemonic, the effects of these factors persist. It seems that having gathered momentum over time, large-scale social and economic processes are not readily abated. In fact, such processes may be accelerating as more haoles and capital arrive in Hawai'i and members of Native Hawaiian and local society experience increasing marginalization (Manicas 1998). Various Native Hawaiian rights and sovereignty movements continue in this context, with potentially momentous but perennially unresolved outcomes and implications.

Capitalism can bring benefits. But, obviously, if one is to engage in the system, it helps to have some capital to start with and to value what that system might provide and how it works. Otherwise, individual long-term economic ascendance is unlikely.

I by no means intend to indicate that people here reject capitalism or its benefits in total. Indeed, many Native Hawaiians and local people of various ethnic backgrounds have died in defense of this nation and its freedoms and best ideals. Nevertheless, many people in Hawai'i move through life without the benefit of inherited capital and without respecting material success that is predicated on the labor of others or a process of outdoing others. Small-boat fishing provides a venue for enjoyment and meaning in life, whereas the world of work often cannot. Yet, under current conditions, it rarely provides a means for significant economic advancement.

But again, there are serious clashes of values here and easy resolution seems improbable. As one of my informants so astutely noted, "People here often make decisions not on how much money it's gonna get 'em, but on the immediate rewards. . . . The [traditional] lifestyle itself is the real reward."

The fishermen I worked with report great satisfaction with the fishing lifestyle in Hawai'i. I know this to be true from observation—the activity brings many nonmonetary benefits. But some of the same folks are divided on whether or not they would recommend fishing as a way of life for their children. People see the dangers of the lifestyle but at the same time have experienced the difficulties of making ends meet through mainstream work. It is also commonly the case that the ugly parts of competitive and aggressive modern American society and culture are seen as something to be rejected. In this context, it can be more sensible to forego the capitalist quest and focus rather on the rich social context of fishing and sharing of resources within the 'ohana and among families in the larger Native Hawaiian and local communities.

The situation begs important questions. Would more favorable economic opportunities and conditions within the predominant economic system lead to the abandonment of tradition in favor of the prospect of material success? Or would such benefits, where guaranteed, be rejected in favor of the traditional, small-scale, and cooperative aspects of the fishing lifestyle? Given the way practitioners of indigenous tradition have reacted elsewhere in the United States, it seems likely that under favorable conditions, practices would be ordered so as to retain the benefits of both systems. But given the momentum of capital in the hands of agents of change in Hawai'i and the historical effects of coastal development elsewhere, it's not clear that fishermen will have the opportunity to fully develop that ideal way of life.

The situation is likely to remain a conundrum for the actors in the modern context because it is so difficult for those without money and power to acquire either, particularly when attention and values are elsewhere. Moreover, agents *with* money and power who might otherwise assist in ensuring a place for traditional life ways and their practitioners are themselves typically involved in other matters, namely moving forward with land development in Hawai'i, often without due consideration of the histories, ideologies, and well-being of so many of its people.

If there is a solution that advocates for the continuation of small-scale work, subsistence, and recreational activities on the ocean amidst the demands of a larger society that constantly reproduces a system requiring competition and commodification of all things, this must be applied in Hawai'i. To solve the conflicts of modern life, Native Hawaiians must experience real political empowerment and the return of a sufficient base of land and sea. Given the effects of history and the conditions of the modern economic climate in Hawai'i, a real solution may also require well-planned application of capital. Without a new and encompassing strategy, Native Hawaiian fishermen will be increasingly challenged in coming years, as will Native Hawaiians and local society in general.

Ideally, fishermen would take part in the design of new strategies. Although membership in an exclusive group has its benefits and differentiating between groups reifies the meaning of membership, a truly adaptive approach on the part of fishermen would involve coalescing at the appropriate times and places to present unified responses to external forces that impinge on the lifestyle in general. In this case, cooperation might lead to the establishment of more viable seafood marketing possibilities, to lobbying efforts for continued access to the ocean, and to strong representation of the fleet(s) when decisions are made regarding management of marine resources in the region. There is no doubt that many fishermen in the region understand this and would move in a unified direction when needed.

Indeed, as migratory pelagic fish stocks in federal and state jurisdiction waters are increasingly managed with regard to international agreements and conservation concerns, representatives of local fleets will likely be forced to defend historical practices. At the time the initial phases of this work were undertaken in 1997, nearly 1,700 small-boat operators fished commercially on a part-time or full-time basis in the Hawaiian Islands. A total of nearly 31,000 commercial trips were reported, resulting in roughly 3,086,000 pounds of fish landed, for an estimated total ex-vessel value of some $4,654,000. The full scope of recreational and subsistence landings and unreported elements of the commercial catch remain unknown. Although the small-boat catch constitutes only a small fraction of pelagic fishing pressure across the Pacific and a small portion of the overall commercial catch in Hawai‘i each year (longline vessel landings typically comprise some 60 percent of total commercial landings), the small-boat fleet arguably does exert some pressure on fish stocks in the Hawai‘i region. If fishing activities associated with different species and ecosystems are increasingly regulated, it can be expected that the flexible nature of small-boat operations here will lead to shifting pursuit and use of available resources. This will require similarly flexible management strategies that are sensitive to the needs and attributes of the fleet. A unified, representative voice may be the best means for ensuring that the small-boat fleet receives due consideration in resource management decisions vis-à-vis other fleets, regions, and nations, based not only on seafood landings or dollar values but also on the full range of social and cultural benefits experienced by the participants.

Given the history of indigenous Hawaiians, certain basic incompatibilities between Native Hawaiian and mainstream haole culture, and the economic vulnerabilities previously described, there is reason to believe that Native Hawaiians may be accorded exceptional consideration in development of future resource management policies. This need not diminish extant or prospective relationships or coalescence between user groups, or diminish the benefits to a more broadly conceived *local* society, also unique in background. Rather this would ideally advocate for perpetuation of customs, traditions, and ways of managing pelagic and other marine resources with roots preceding by many centuries the arrival of other peoples on these Islands.[1]

[1]The Western Pacific Fishery Management Council has developed and is implementing programs intended to meet these objectives. These include a Community Development Program (CDP) and a Community Demonstration Project Program (CDPP). The CDP calls for increased representation of indigenous persons in fisheries managed by the Council, and the CDPP is a funding program that promotes traditional indigenous fishing practices.

Why on their own ‘āina (land) shouldn't Native Hawaiians seek to practice traditional ways, combine them with positive aspects of modernity, and create a new way of living as they see fit? Hawaiians speak for themselves on these issues, of course, but the social scientist with a conscience cannot avoid asking, "Has the dominant political economy been so successful and without deleterious social consequence that no other possibility should ever be tried or supported?" and answering, "Obviously it has not been without such effect, as the history and modern state of affairs of many indigenous peoples in the United States make clear." Insofar as this nation was founded on the principles of innovation and the freedom of its people to aspire, perhaps its true magnanimity will be evinced in willingness to actively support indigenous persons and small societies seeking to chart a new way of life without denying the values or practices of the old.

> Arriving at the harbor at 5:20 a.m. with just a hint of daylight peeking over the green pali, I notice there's already a line of vessels at the access ramp—over 40 vessels are lined up to enter the water—a Saturday crowd.
>
> The harbor office lights are on, and people are already milling about. Uncle Saul steps out of the office and looks toward the mountains, breathing deeply the sweet early morning air of Hawai‘i. Thick clouds billow over the mountains. It is raining lightly over the harbor, promising a rainbow as soon as the sun clears the horizon. A light east-northeast breeze gently ruffles the surface, and a slight surge gently rocks the boats in their moorings.
>
> It will be a good day for fishing. Despite a long history of challenges and an uncertain future for his people, the kupuna smiles, deeply.

Glossary of Hawaiian Terms and Phrases*

A

'ahi n. yellowfin tuna, an important fish in the Honolulu market. Said to derive from smoke and fire resulting from the fishing line chafing along the gunwale of the canoe as the fish quickly carries the line underwater.

āholehole n. juvenile stage of the endemic āhole, Hawaiian flagtail fish. Lives in both fresh and salt water. Once used for ceremonial purposes, loves magic and to chase away evil spirits.

ahupua'a n. land division usually extending from the uplands to the sea.

'āina n. land, earth, especially of Hawai'i.

akamai nvs. smart, clever, expert; smartness, skill, wit; especially savvy.

aku n. bonita or skipjack tuna.

akule n. big-eyed or goggle-eyed scad fish. Frequently caught above mounds of coral reef (see *ko'a*).

ali'i nvs. chiefly nobility.

aloha nvt., nvs. love, affection, compassion, mercy, sympathy, pity, kindness, sentiment, grace, charity. An expression of affection offered at meeting and departure.

ama n. stabilizing float portion of the outrigger canoe, attached to its 'iako or extending arms.

a'u n. Marlin.

E

'ehu kai n. sea spray, generated by offshore wind blowing against breaking waves, visible many hundreds of feet in the atmosphere during large swells.

H

haka lele n. altar platform.

haku n. master.

hālau n. long house, as used for storing canoes, for hula instruction, and community meetings.

hana pa'a vt. to make secure, fasten; to hook a fish.

haole nvs. formerly, any foreigner; foreign, introduced, of foreign origin. Now, typically white person, American, Englishman, Caucasian: *Ho'o haole*: To act like a white person, or assume airs of superiority. *Ho'o haole 'ia*: Americanized, Europeanized; to have become like a white person or have adopted the ways of the white man.

hapa nvs. of mixed blood, person of mixed blood, as in *hapa haole.*

heiau n. place of worship, shrine, typically constructed from lava rock.

holoholo vi. to go for a ride, walk, or sail; out for pleasure, stroll, promenade; recreation. Euphemism for going fishing.

ho'olaulea n. celebration

hui n. club, association, society.

hukilau nvi. a seine net; to fish with the seine, typically requiring cooperation of villagers.

huli-huli v. literally, to turn-turn, as a rotisserie. Also used in the vernacular to refer to poultry or other meat that has been grilled with such a device.

humuhumunukunukuāpua'a n. state fish; rhinecanthus

I

'iako n. the arms of an outrigger canoe, attached to the body of the canoe at its base and to the *ama* or float at its terminal end.

K

kāhala n. amberjack or yellowtail.

kalo n. Taro (*Colocasia esculenta*); tuberous, starchy edible root.

*Etymology and definitions of Hawaiian words and phrases derive in large part from the 1986 edition of the *Hawaiian Dictionary, Revised and Enlarged Edition,* Mary Kawena Pukui and Samuel H. Elbert (Eds.). Honolulu: University of Hawaii Press. The reader is referred to pp. xvii–xviii of this source for a guide to pronunciation of Hawaiian.

kamaʻāina nvi. native-born, especially of Hawaiʻi; and/or one who is closely acquainted or highly familiar with Hawaiʻi.

kanaka nvs. human being, person.

kanaka maoli n. native Hawaiian, indigenous person of Hawaiʻi.

kapu nvs. taboo, prohibition; special privilege or exemption from ordinary taboo; sacredness; prohibited, forbidden.

kaukau n., v. local term with uncertain etymology, meaning both food and eating.

keiki nvi. child, offspring, descendant, progeny.

kiawe n. Mesquite (*Prosopis pallida*); noxious thorny shrub introduced in 1828 by Father Bachelot, first Catholic priest in Hawaiʻi.

koʻa nvs. Coral, coral head; n. Fishing grounds, usually identified by lining up with points along the shore or in the mountains.

koa haole (*Leucaena leucocephala*); common roadside shrub or small tree introduced from tropical America; nuisance.

kōkua nvt. help, aid, cooperative assistance.

konohiki n. person in charge of an ahupuaʻa, component thereof; land or fishing rights were often under the control of a konohiki.

kuleana nvt. right, privilege, concern, responsibility, title.

kupuna n. grandparent, ancestor, relative or close friend of the grandparent's generation, grandaunt, granduncle; person of wisdom and status.

L

lānai n. Porch, veranda, balcony, terrace.

lau nvi. leaf, frond, leaflet, greens.

laulima nvi. cooperation, joint action; group of people working together; community food patch; to work together, cooperate. *Lit.,* many hands.

lawaiʻa nvi. fisherman; fishing technique; to fish, to catch fish.

leina a ka ʻuhane – n. place where the spirits leap to the nether world.

limu n. a general name for all kinds of plants living under water, both fresh and salt, also algae growing in any damp place in the air, as on the ground, on rocks, and on other plants.

loa nvs. long, tall, far, permanent.

lōkahi nvs. unity, agreement, accord, unison, harmony.

loko iʻa n. fish pond.

lolo crazy.

lūʻau feast; formerly *pāʻina.*

M

mahalo nui loa nvt. an expression of great thanks; literally, thank you large and long.

mahimahi n. dolphin, a game fish up to 1.5 meters long, popular for food.

maikaʻi nvs. goodness, righteousness, good.

makai n. Ocean; reference to the direction of the ocean.

makua kāne n. father, uncle, male cousin of parents' generation.

mālama nvt. to take care of, tend, attend, care for, preserve, protect, beware, save, maintain.

malihini nvs. stranger, newcomer, tourist, company; unfamiliar with a place or custom.

mālolo n. general term for flying fishes in Hawaiʻi.

manini n. common reef surgeonfish, also called convict tang in mature stage. Now sometimes used to infer diminutive size, small.

mauka n. inland, toward the uplands or mountains.

N

naʻauao nvs. wisdom, learned, enlightened.

nuku n. mouth; entrance to a harbor

O

ʻohana nvs. family, relative, kin group; related.

ʻōkole n. gluteus maximus.

olonā n. a native shrub, with large, ovate, fine-toothed leaves, related to the māmaki. Formerly, the bark was valued highly as the source of a strong, durable fiber for fishing nets and line.

onaga n. red snapper.

ono – n. large mackerel-type fish, also known as wahoo. Also means delicious.

ʻōpelu n. Mackerel scad.

ʻopihi n. Limpets. Found in the intertidal zone.

P

pāhoehoe nvt. lava that cooled in smooth, unbroken sheets, common along many areas of the Big Island.

pāʻina nvt. meal, dinner, small party with dinner.

pākuʻikuʻi n. a surgeonfish, good eating.

palapala hōʻike n. report, reporting document.

pali n. cliff, precipice, precipitous ridgeline.

palu ʻahi n. method of fishing for tuna wherein a weighted bag containing chopped bait and baited hook is lowered to by hand line. At the proper depth, the line is jerked, thereby releasing the slipknot securing the bag. The contents are spilled, ideally incurring a feeding reaction by the tuna.

pau vs. finished, ended, through, terminated, completed, over, all done.

pau hana nvs. end of work, end of the workday or week.

pili ana n. connection.

pōhaku n. rock, stone, mineral, tablet

poke nvt. to slice, cut crosswise into pieces, as fish or wood. Cubed fish served with various condiments such as shoyu, seaweed, and so forth.

poʻonui n. pacific big-eye tuna.

pōpolo n. black nightshade (*Solanum nigrum*). Vernacular, persons of African ancestry.

pua kenikeni n. shrub or small tree for its foliage, flowers, and fruit. The fragrant flowers are typically about 5 cm long and are often used for leis.

puka n. hole or perforation.

puʻu n. any kind of small protuberance; hill.

U

uhu n. Parrotfish.

ulua n. certain species of crevalle, jack, trevaly, or pompano, an important game fish and food item; immature individual is called a papio.

W

waʻa pā n. three-board outrigger canoe.

wahine n. woman, Hawaiian woman.

References

Abbott, Isabella. 1999. Personal communication. Department of Botany, University of Hawaii at Manoa. Honolulu.

Adler, Patricia, and Peter Adler. 2004. *Paradise Laborers—Hotel Work in the Global Economy*. Ithaca, NY, and London: Cornell University Press.

Buckley, R. M., D. G. Itano, and T. W. Buckley. 1989. Fish Aggregation Device (FAD) Enhancement of Offshore Fisheries in American Samoa. *Bulletin of Marine Science* 44(2):942–949.

Churchill, Ward, and Sharon H. Venne (eds.). 2005. *Islands in Captivity—The International Tribunal on the Rights of Indigenous Hawaiians*. Lilikala Kame'eleihiwa, Hawaiian language editor. Cambridge, MA: South End Press.

Corney, Peter. 1896. *Voyages in the Northern Pacific, 1813–1818*. Honolulu: Thomas G. Thrum.

Culliney, John. 1988. *Islands in a Far Sea*. San Francisco: Sierra Club Books.

Davis, Dona Lee, and Jane Nadel-Klein. 1988. Terra Cognita?: A Review of the Literature. In *To Work and to Weep: Women in Fishing Economies*. J. Nadel-Klein and D.L. Davis (eds.), pp. 18–51. St. John's: ISER Books, Memorial University, Newfoundland.

Fielding, Ann, and Ed Robinson. 1987. *An Underwater Guide to Hawai'i*. Honolulu: University of Hawai'i Press.

Giddens, Anthony. 1984. *The Constitution of Society—Outline of the Theory of Structuration*. Cambridge: Polity Press.

Goodluck, Charlotte T., and Angela A. A. Willeto. 2001. *Native American Kids 2001: Indian Children's Well-Being Indicators Data Book*. National Indian Child Welfare Association. Casey Family Programs. Seattle.

Goto, Akira. 1986. *Prehistoric Ecology and Economy of Fishing in Hawai'i: An Ethnoarchaeological Approach*. Ph.D. dissertation in Anthropology. University of Hawai'i. Honolulu.

Hamilton, Marcia S. 1998. Cost-Earnings Study of Hawaii's Charter Fishing, 1996–1997. *SOEST Publication 98-08, JIMAR Contribution 98-32*. University of Hawai'i at Manoa, and National Marine Fisheries Service, Honolulu Laboratory. Honolulu.

Hamilton, Marcia S., and Stephen W. Huffman. 1997. *Cost-Earnings Study of Hawai'i's Small Boat Fishery*. SOEST 97-06. JIMAR Contribution 97-314. University of Hawai'i at Manoa, and National Marine Fisheries Service, Honolulu Laboratory. Honolulu.

Hamilton, Marcia S., Rita E. Curtis, and Michael D. Travis. 1997. *Cost-Earnings Study of the Hawai'i-Based Domestic Longline Fleet*. SOEST 96-03. JIMAR Contribution 96-300. University of Hawai'i at Manoa, and National Marine Fisheries Service, Honolulu Laboratory. Honolulu.

Hawai'i Fishing News. 2005. Available online at: http://www.Hawaiifishingnews.com/records

Hoffman, Robert G., and Hiroshi Yamauchi. 1972. *Recreational Fishing in Hawai'i and its Economic Impact on the State and Local Economies*. College of Tropical Agriculture, Hawai'i Agricultural Experiment Station, University of Hawai'i, Departmental Paper. Honolulu.

Humphries, Robert. 1999. Personal Communication. Fishery Biologist. National Marine Fisheries Service, Honolulu Laboratory.

I'i, Jon Papa. 1973. *Fragments of Hawai'ian History*. As recorded by John Papa I'i sometime after the mid-19th century. Translated by Mary Kawena Pukui. Honolulu: Bishop Museum Press.

International Game Fish Association. 2006. *World Recod Game Fishes*. Fishing Hall of Fame and Museum. Dania Beach, FL.

Itano, David. 1995. Small Boat Pelagic Fisheries: A Review of FAD Utilization in the Pacific Island Region. In *Achieving Goals for Sustainable Living in the Aquatic Environment. Toward a Pacific Island-Based Tuna Industry*. D. G. Malcolm, Jr., Jeanne Skog, and Diane Zachary (eds.). The Fifth Conference/ Workshop, Cultural Values in the Age of Technology. Presented by the Maui Pacific Center: Kihei.

Kirch, Patrick V. 1985. *Feathered Gods and Fishhooks: An Introduction to Hawai'ian Archaeology and Prehistory*. Honolulu: University of Hawai'i Press.

Maly, Kepa, and Onaona Maly. 2003. *Ka Hana Lawai'a A Me Na Ko'a O Na Kai 'Ewalu. A history of Fishing Practices and Marine Fisheries of the Hawai'ian Islands.* Kumu Pono Associates. Prepared for the Nature Conservancy and Kamehameha Schools. Hilo.

Manicas, Peter. 1998. *The Los Angelisation of Hawai'i.* Paper presented at the 1998 meetings of the Hawai'i Sociological Association. Department of Sociology. University of Hawai'i at Manoa. Honolulu.

Matsuoka, Jon, Davianna McGregro, Luciano Minerbi, and Malia Akutagawa. 1994. *Governor's Moloka'i Subsistence Task Force Final Report.* University of Hawai'i and Ke Kua'Aina Hanauna Hou. Prepared for the Moloka'i Subsistence Task Force and the State of Hawai'i, Department of Business, Economic Development, and Tourism. Honolulu.

McGoodwin, James R. 1990. *Crisis in the World's Fisheries.* Stanford: Stanford University Press.

Nelson, Victoria. 1989. *My Time in Hawai'i—A Polynesian Memoir.* New York: St. Martin's Press.

Nordyke, Eleanor C. 1989. *The Peopling of Hawai'i.* Second Edition. Honolulu: University of Hawai'i Press.

Office of Hawaiian Affairs. 2002. *Native Hawaiian Data Book.* Available online at: http://www.oha.org/pdf/databook_6_02.pdf

Rizzuto, Jim. 1987. *Fishing Hawai'i Style. Volume 2. A Guide to Saltwater Angling.* Honolulu: Fishing Hawai'i Style Ltd., a subsidiary of Hawai'i Fishing News.

Sahlins, Marshall. 1989. Captain Cook at Hawai'i. *Journal of the Polynesian Society* 86:371–423.

Schug, Donald. 2001. Hawai'i's Commercial Fishing Industry: 1820–1945. *The Hawai'ian Journal of History* 35:15–34. Honolulu.

———. 2002. Personal Communication. Fisheries Consultant. Davis, CA, and Honolulu.

Scobie, Richard. 1949. *The Technology and Economics of Fishing in Relationship to Hawai'ian Culture.* M.A. thesis. London School of Economics.

Severance, Craig J. 2001. Big Fish from Small Boats: Challenge, Competition and Camaraderie in Hawaii Small-Scale Trolling Tournaments. In Miller, Marc L., Charles Daxboeck, Christopher Dahl, Kevin Kelly, and Paul Dalzell (eds.). Proceedings of the 1998 Pacific Island Gamefish Symposium. Honolulu: Western Pacific Regional Fishery Management Council.

Shomura, Richard. 1987. *Hawai'i's Marine Fisheries Resources: Yesterday (1900), and Today (1986).* Southwest Fisheries Center Administrative Report H-87-21. NOAA. Honolulu.

Squire, James L., Jr. 1976. *List of Fishing Clubs Interested in Marine Angling in Southern California, Central and Northern California, and the Hawai'ian Islands.* National Marine Fisheries Service Administrative Report LJ-76-14. NOAA. Honolulu.

Squire, James L., Jr., and Susan E. Smith. 1977. *Angler's Guide to the United States Pacific Coast. Marine Fish, Fishing Grounds, and Facilities.* Department of Commerce, NOAA. Seattle.

Thiessen, Victor, Anthony Davis, and Sven Jentoft. 1992. The Veiled Crew: An Exploratory Study of Wives' Reported and Desired Contributions to Coastal Fisheries Enterprises in Northern Norway and Nova Scotia. *Human Organization* 51(4).

Tuggle, H. D., R. Cordy, and M. Child. 1978. Volcanic Glass Hydration-Ring Age Determination for Bellows Dune, Hawai'i. *New Zealand Archaeological Association Newsletter* 21:57–77.

Index